THE LAST UP

A Curious Tale About the Future of Sales

by

Jimmy Vee & Travis Miller
- with Dan Clements -

DEDICATED TO THE
ULTIMATE COACH, AND
OUR DEAR FRIEND —
ROB BERKLEY.

CONTENTS

CଃV଼ଓ

CHAPTER 1

THE GORILLA

I am sweating my balls off.

Or, more accurately, I would be sweating my balls off if I actually had any.

Okay. I have balls. Literally. But figuratively speaking? As in courage? Bravado? Cojones? If I had those kinds of balls, I wouldn't be standing on a sidewalk in a monkey suit. If I had those kinds of balls, I'd have drawn the line long ago.

If I had those kinds of balls, I'd be working somewhere else.

So, figuratively, I have no balls. But the monkey suit is real. I'm actually wearing it. It's 98 degrees out here, but inside the suit, it's more like 110. The tiny slice of the world I can see through the eye holes of the rubber mask is a stinging blur of sweat and heat waves rising off the asphalt.

That's pretty much how this starts: I'm standing on the shoulder of a busy street dressed as a monkey, waving my arms up and down in the summer heat, just like I have for the past three days.

And I'm actually still showing up for work every day.

My name is Mark Dunham, and I sell cars.

At least, that's my job description, but it feels like someone else's most of the time. I've only been on the job a few weeks, and if I really sold cars, well, I probably would have actually sold some by now. Right?

⁎

I've only been back inside the dealership for five minutes, guzzling water and mashing my face against the air conditioner vent, when I hear the grating southern drawl:

"Yo, Bubbles. No ups on the lot. Time to do your thing."

That's Earl Cochrane talking. He's kind of a jerk.

He's been here since the Stone Age, and he thinks he's God's gift to car sales.

It was Earl's idea to get the damn gorilla. If you pass within five miles of Langford Auto Sales, you can't miss it. Picture an inflatable ape, 60 feet high. When the wind blows, it looks like it's beating its chest. Earl got a deal on it. By "deal" I mean he got them to throw in the monkey suit for free. After the setup crew wrestled the gorilla onto the roof and got it tethered and inflated, Earl handed me the monkey suit and kicked me outside to bring in some ups. I've been out there for three days straight.

"Earl. It's 100 degrees out there. I'm dying."

"Yeah. Well, Koko's still working." Koko is what Earl calls the big gorilla. "He never takes a break. That's the power of advertising, son. It never quits." Earl puts all the emphasis on the first syllable. AD-vertising. Like he discovered it himself.

Koko. Bubbles. Is this what I get from four years of college and a decade of work?

"Go on." Earl has his feet up on his desk. "We need some ups." Earl holds a folded newspaper in his hand. He was reading it, but now he's actually fanning himself with it.

What a jerk. I should stand up to him. I should tell

him to shove the monkey suit up his plaid-painted ass.

But I can't.

First of all, as previously discussed, I don't have the balls. I'm not really the in-your-face kind.

Second, we really do need the ups. Ups are what we call prospects—people who walk onto the lot looking for a vehicle. No ups means no sales, and we need more sales. Plenty more, or Langford Auto is going to have one more in a string of slow months.

Plenty more or none of us are going to make any real money.

***

Langford Auto Sales is mostly one big open showroom. Old Henry "Hank" Langford, the founder, didn't believe in private offices. He was an enlisted man in the Second World War, hated rank, and came home determined to prove he was as good as any officer.

And prove it he did. He started the business on this very spot and rode the car wave of the fifties like he was born for it.

Today, the sales desks are still pushed up near the back wall all around the main showroom, just like they were in the fifties. The sales guys—Earl, Rusty,

Trevor, and me—sit at desks that are all equal in size. All equal in stature. Just the way Henry liked it.

Of course, that's never the way things work in real life. Our desks are the same, but that's where the similarities end. Where Earl has his boots up on his desk, fanning himself with the paper, Rusty's feet are flat on the floor, his nose practically touching his desk as he pours over brochures and specs for the latest models. It's almost as if he and Earl are physically inverted.

Trevor, on the other hand, is Earl's emotional inverse. Earl will ask anyone for a sale, or anything else for that matter. Trevor won't ask anyone for anything, ever—with the possible exception of advice. He's the most introverted salesperson on the planet. He spends most of his day with his nose in a mystery novel, and I'm sure he misses his draw every month.

But there we all sit in a democratic row—at the same desks, on the same days, at the same business—right out in the open where we take turns waiting for ups to hit the lot, so we can try our hand at selling cars.

Still, for all this so-called democracy, so far I'm the only one who has to wear the monkey suit.

The only private offices belong to the accountant, Claire, and to Henry's son, Alan. I suspect Henry would have blown a gasket if he'd seen his son, the current president, in a private office away from the action. But Alan's not like Henry. For one thing, Alan's not a born people person like Henry was. He's a numbers guy. The MBA type. I suspect that's why he converted the old parts room into an office after Henry died. He likes to hide a bit. He's smart—don't get me wrong—but he tends to stay off the floor.

Plus, I just don't know if Alan loves cars. Henry had a love affair with cars. You can see it in every picture hanging in the showroom. He didn't pick this business just to make money. He picked it like he was picking a bride for life, which, in the end, the dealership turned out to be. Henry worked this place until the day he died. It was a til-death-do-us-part relationship, literally.

Henry loved cars, and he loved people. That's a powerful combination.

***

I'm making it sound like I knew Henry, but I didn't. I'm the new guy, and Henry was long gone before I got here. But if you're a smart new guy, you pay attention. You look around. I've had enough jobs to know that. And when you look around Langford Auto, you see Henry everywhere. He's in practically every photo on every wall. A grinning Henry shaking hands with President Eisenhower. A grinning Henry cutting the ribbon at Langford's grand opening. A grinning Henry being dropped in the dunk tank on family day at the dealership.

A lot of grinning Henry. Alan does less of that. As does everyone around here, it seems, myself included. With sales as slow as they've been, smiles are few and far between.

Henry's in our conversations with customers too. Some of the older ones still talk about all the cars they bought from "Hank."

But for all the evidence of Henry "Hank" Langford on the walls, the man himself is long gone. And lately, it's like the glory days of car sales are gone with him. Lost to the past, just like Henry himself.

I shouldn't complain. I like cars, and I like people—just like Henry did. But that doesn't seem to have taken me far. Alan basically abandoned me on the floor with Earl my first day here. And you know where that's gotten me: dry humping the air conditioner and wishing it was time to go home.

Ironically, though, home is the reason I'm here. It's

the reason I'm climbing back into the damn monkey suit and heading into the blast furnace that is the outside world. Not because Earl "God's-Gift-To-Sales" Cochrane is telling me to, but because my wife, Charlotte, is the daughter of the owner of the largest dealership in the state, a couple of hundred miles away.

Yep. My father-in-law got me this job. Near as I can figure, he did it because: (a) I didn't have one—I'd just lost my so-called professional job; (b) because he knows Alan, and he knew Henry; and, mostly, (c) because Charlotte asked him to.

In Charlotte's mind, I'm being groomed to take over the family business. I don't know what's on her father's mind, but either way, I'm feeling some serious pressure to perform.

It all adds up to one thing: when you feel like your marriage and your mortgage and your future are on the line, you try harder. Even if that means dressing as a monkey.

CHAPTER 2

THE CELLAR

I ignore Earl's smirk—which I know is there but can't see because of the mask—and head for the door. I pass the reception counter on the way.

Jennifer, the receptionist, is eyeing me skeptically. She has the look of someone watching a train wreck on television: mildly disturbed but not about to change the channel or anything crazy like that.

"Are you going to be okay out there?" Her eyebrows indicate mild disbelief.

"I'll be fine," I say. My voice is muffled, and I hope that fills it with a bravado I definitely don't feel.

I step outside.

Oh my God.

The heat is . . . I can't describe it.

But I am most certainly not going to be fine.

***

I wait for the shock to subside—for my body to adjust to the heat—but . . . it doesn't. It's as if I've walked into a blast furnace that's actually forging the neat rows of cars that surround me.

I'm about to turn around and go inside, and then I remember Earl's smirk. Screw him. I'm not giving in that easily.

I ignore the stinging sweat that's already running into my eyes and pick up my props: an enormous stuffed banana and a large sign on a wooden picket. We've gone bananas with our low prices!!!!

The idea is as simple as it is terrible. My job is to scamper up and down the shoulder of the main road fronting the lot, waving my banana and hoisting the sign. That way, anyone who doesn't notice the 60-foot gorilla on the roof of the building—the blind, perhaps—might see me and say, "Dolores, I only buy cars from places with monkeys, so I guess this is our spot."

It's ridiculous. And so I do what I normally do when

faced with humiliation: I give in. I tuck the banana under my arm, hoist the sign over my shoulder, and prepare to take on the world. Or at least the sidewalk.

Someone must be punishing me. That's the only explanation left. Being slowly cooked to death in a monkey suit is my penance for blowing the last three ups I've had this week.

With the first up, I tried to be a salesman like Earl's been "teaching" me. I tried to sell her a car, but she left almost before I could finish my pitch. With the second, I tried to impress him with my product knowledge, à la Rusty, but I'm pretty sure when he left, he was more confused than when he got here. Rumor has it that he ended up buying a car down the street that same day.

With the last up, I tried to play it cool and act nonchalant, like I didn't care if they bought a car or not. No pressure, right?

No sale either.

I tried all the techniques I'd learned from the other guys who work here, but they all led to the same result. As they say, three strikes; you're out. And in my case, out meant outside in this absurd monkey suit.

I grip my sign, sigh, and head for the roadside.

That's when I realize I've been standing in

the shade.

I've just stepped out from the building's shadow into full afternoon sun, and I feel my blood pressure go through the roof. More sweat—if that's even possible—starts to run down my face and body. It's so hot that the rubber of the mask feels like it's burning the tips of my ears.

I look ahead and focus my attention on the lone tree near the edge of the road. It's casting a cool, dark shadow onto the grass.

Salvation. If I can get there, I can pound the sign into the grass and stay in the shade. Maybe even swing from the tree a bit. For effect.

I squint against the salty sweat in my eyes and walk between the first row of cars with their window stickers, trying to focus on the cool relief of the tree in the distance.

I make it about 40 feet—just past a Cadillac that's been on the lot for weeks—and I feel like I'm starting to adjust to the heat. I guess I'm adapting.

Then my legs buckle, and I fold at the knees. I tip sideways like a prize-fighter taking a dive. Just like that.

My first thought is embarrassment. I try to jump back up hoping no one saw me, but my legs simply aren't working. I feel fine, more or less. But no legs. I can move my gorilla arms, even do a bit of a push up as if I'm about to get up, but it's like I'm paralyzed below the waist.

Then, the heat hits me again. Like a huge, hot blanket falling on me. And now I'm scared.

I turn my head to call for help, but I've fallen alongside the Cadillac, out of view. Unless someone saw me fall, no one knows I'm here.

I try to push myself into the open—back in the direction I fell from—but I don't have the strength to push my whole body backward. So I settle for crawling forward, which I can do by dragging myself along with my elbows.

After a few shuffles and grunts, I reach the back of the Cadillac. Then the thirst hits me. Someone has filled my mouth with dust. Crackers. Cement. Sand. I'm dry beyond dry, parched beyond parched.

I look around the back of the Cadillac, and I can see a row of rear bumpers extending toward the corner of the building. Toward cool, sweet shade.

I turn and start my elbow shuffle again. One car. Then another. I realize that my trajectory is going to take me past the corner of the building, out of sight, but that's fine. I'll be able to regain my composure in the shade, and then go back inside.

I only have three cars to go when I feel my arms start to weaken. They're fading out just the way my legs did. And that's when the thought occurs to me:

I'm going to die out here behind some random car, wearing a gorilla suit.

The thought spurs me on.

I shuffle on my elbows past another car. I'm nearly there. I realize that at some point, I've stopped sweating. I don't think that's good. I think back to what I know about heat stroke and dehydration. Not much, but I'm almost positive it's not good when you stop sweating.

Or is it good? I can't remember.

I realize I've passed the last car, and now I'm beside the building. I've actually gone farther than I needed to, and I turn again, dragging my useless legs toward the vague shape of the showroom. Between my delirium and the mask, I can just make out dark shade. That's what I need: cool, dark, life-saving shade. I drop my head down and make an elbow sprint for safety.

Before I can reach it, my head slams into something hard, and I nearly black out. I reach to rub it and for the first time realize that I can just take the damn mask off.

I yank it from my head and discover that I've crawled right into the cement front edge of the storm cellar doors that extend from the north side of the building and open upward. They're preventing me from reaching the shade.

But they're doing something else too. They're blowing cool air on my face.

Like a tiny air conditioner, the crack between the doors is letting a sliver of cool air out to tease the skin on my face.

Right now, what I want most in the whole world—more than shade, more than water, more than a cold drink full of ice served to me in a bathtub of cool water—is more of that cool air.

Without thinking, I drag myself up to my knees and grasp the handle of the storm cellar door. Praying the door isn't locked, I jerk it upward. It surges open, and the momentum swings it to the side where it hangs, tethered by a short length of chain.

I can feel the cool air below like a still pool. Balancing on my knees, I peer over the lip of the stairs that lead down into darkness.

Then dizziness overwhelms me, and I pitch forward.

I'm dimly aware of stairs and some pain. And then

the door slams shut above me. As I fall like a stone into cool, dark, deep silence, one last thought flashes through my mind.

There's gotta be a better way to sell cars.

And then nothing.

***

It's pitch black.

I open my eyes.

It's still pitch black.

Maybe the power is out. I hope I haven't slept through the alarm. Charlotte will be pissed.

I reach out to find the clock on my bedside table, and my hand brushes something coarse and hairy . . .

My heart leaps, and I jerk my arm back.

But then I realize what I've grabbed: the mask.

It all comes back to me. I'm in the storm cellar.

What an idiot I am. I'll be the laughingstock of the dealership. I say a brief prayer of hope that I haven't been unconscious long and then stand up. My legs, I'm relieved to discover, seem to be working again.

It's dark. Really dark. I turn in a circle, looking for light from the crack between the storm cellar doors, but there's nothing. Just blackness.

It smells musty. Dank.

I hold my hands out in front of me and gradually feel my way forward. Something brushes my face and scares the crap out of me. I bat it away, but it gets caught on my hand, and I realize it's a string. The kind connected to a light.

I pull it, and the lights come on.

And I scream as I realize that Henry "Hank" Langford is standing right there.

***

I'm choking off the scream even as it leaves my mouth. It's not Henry, summoned back to life, but a life-sized cardboard cut out. Like a movie promo piece.

Unlike the framed photos I've seen in the dealership, though, Cardboard Henry is wearing what looks like a baseball jersey and ball cap. His shirt has "Langford" in stylish script across the chest. Dangling from his neck is a silver coach's whistle. Must be a marketing piece from some little league team Henry sponsored. I'm reminded again of how much greater a role the dealership used to play in this community.

As my heart rate settles to normal, I turn away from Coach Langford and look around the cellar. It's a typical basement. Low ceiling. Dusty. Musty. Rough concrete floor, damp in the corners from the last rain.

There's a bunch of cardboard boxes, stacked on skids to keep them off the wet floor. Henry's not so lucky: his cardboard feet and base are damp and peeling up to his shins.

"You've got a bit of a lean there, Hank," I say out loud. No answer. He looks kind of unhappy. Maybe it's just the humidity in the cardboard.

The instant I think humidity, my thirst returns. I feel an immediate, urgent need to drink, and I turn to leave.

Then I stop. I wonder if I should move Henry. It feels . . . irreverent somehow to leave him to slowly mold and bend and flake away in the cellar.

Yes. I should move him. Move him and then get upstairs and back to work and hope no one noticed I was gone.

I pick Henry up and lean him over the palettes of boxes. I set him down gently—more gently, I realize, than an old wet piece of cardboard really deserves—and I notice the boxes are labeled. One catches my eye: "The Last Up" is written on it in felt marker.

I fold back the flaps of the box and look inside. It's full of round canisters, as well as a larger, square box.

I lift the lid off the larger box. It's a film projector, packed neatly in old newspapers, the reel arms folded down at its sides. The canisters, I realize, must be old 16 mm film cans. Old movies, or something. There are six of them in total, each numbered.

I grab the top one. It's labeled "The Last Up. Part 1: The Problem with Selling Cars."

"Hank," I say out loud, "I could have written the screenplay for that one."

I'm so funny. I laugh out loud and then look over to see if I've cheered Henry up. That's when a part of me realizes I really need to rehydrate. I'm starting to lose it.

When I see Cardboard Henry grinning at me, I realize I've lost it altogether. I drop the film can with a clatter. I look down at it, then back at Henry. His face is back to how it was. Glum. Dejected.

I really need to get some water.

I stoop to pick up the can, and when I stand up again, Cardboard Henry is grinning right at me.

My spine shivers and goose bumps march across my back.

I turn and bolt for the exit.

I fly up the stairs, throw open the storm cellar doors, and practically leap out onto the asphalt parking lot.

It's only then that I realize three things:

The first is that I've left the light on downstairs.

The second is that it's dark outside. The light from the cellar is spilling out into the lot. I was down there for hours.

The third, the one that I don't even realize until I reach my car, is that I'm still clutching the film canister.

CHAPTER 3

THE FILM

Morning arrives like someone driving a nail through my face.

The pain in my head is so severe that I don't even attempt to open my eyes for a full five minutes.

Even with my eyes closed, the world is a hazy red, and it takes a moment for me to realize why: it's daylight out. I don't know what time it is, but it's never this bright when I wake up for work. I am late.

I ease my eyes open and turn my head very slowly to the left. Charlotte's side of the bed is empty. As I try to shift her pillow out of the way, so I can see the clock on the bedside table, a black, hairy mass emerges into sight.

It's my arm. I'm still wearing the gorilla suit.

Everything floods back. The heat, the cellar, the dehydration. And the concussion, apparently.

I've got to get to work. As if the whole thing isn't embarrassing enough already, I'm now late. In fact, I realize, I've been MIA since yesterday afternoon when I walked out the door of the dealership and collapsed in the heat.

I sit up. The pain in my head nearly knocks me over. But with some effort, I stand; then I look down to discover that in addition to the chimp suit, I'm still wearing my shoes. I must have walked into the house and fallen straight into bed.

On my bedside table is a huge pitcher with a few ounces of water in the bottom. At least I had the presence of mind to drink something before I fell asleep—quite possibly my only sensible act in the last 24 hours. Even so, I am thirsty beyond belief. I head for the kitchen.

***

Charlotte is gone. There's a terse note on the kitchen table. She apparently thinks I was out drinking, philandering, or stealing from orphans last night. At any rate, she is "out" and will be back "at some point."

I drink what feels like a gallon of water. Thirty head-splitting minutes later, I've swapped the gorilla suit for a shower and human clothes, and I am driving to the office. I try to avoid the rear-view mirror—partly out of shame, but mostly because I look like someone actually did drive a nail through my face. There's a nasty scrape on one cheek, and my eye is a light shade of purple, courtesy of my fall down the stairs.

If nothing else, I'll at least have a good excuse for not selling anything today. Again.

***

Thankfully, Earl and Trevor are outside the dealership service bay talking to one of the mechanics. I'll be able to park and slip inside without facing an inquisition.

I glance at the cellar doors warily as I walk around to the front of the building. In the light of day—and in light of my concussion—the night before feels more silly than scary.

As I pass the reception counter, Jennifer's eyes widen. "Morning," I say brightly, breezing past her and heading straight for my desk as quickly as I can.

"Alan wants to see you," she says.

My hopes of putting all this behind me vanish.

I knock on Alan's door and stick my head partway through the doorway, trying to keep the scraped and bruised side of my face out of view.

"Come in and close the door, Mark," Alan says. He's looking off to the side, staring at a spreadsheet on his computer screen.

I do as instructed and take a seat in front of his desk. Alan turns to face me.

"Thanks for . . . " he trails off when he sees my face. His mouth moves as if he's about to comment, but he just sighs and leans back in his chair. "How's it going out there?" he asks.

"Good. There are some people out front." I don't mention that those people are Earl and Trevor.

"That's good. That's really good."

"Uh . . . yeah. It's really good," I say. "It's really . . . really good."

There's an uncomfortable pause.

"Is everything okay, Mark?" he finally asks.

"Oh sure. It's great. The guys are really helping me out. You know . . . on the sales side."

He looks over at his spreadsheet. "I wanted to talk

to you about that. You don't really have any numbers on the board."

"I guess I'm kind of the low man on the totem pole."

"They're not splitting ups with you?" he says, suddenly alert.

"No, they are. I guess I just need a little more practice, maybe."

Behind Alan there's a large picture of Henry. In it, he's leaning against the huge hood of a shiny 1950 Packard with his arms folded, looking like the king of the universe. He looks exactly like he does in the cardboard cutout, and I wonder if it was taken at the same time. I feel a small shiver run down my spine.

"Beautiful car," I say, motioning to the picture. "Probably be worth a fortune now."

"Not that one," Alan says bluntly, without looking away from his screen. Then he looks up. "I'm just going to be straight with you," he says.

Uh oh.

"We need to get the numbers up," he continues. "Not just you—everyone." He taps his keyboard and squints at the spreadsheet. "Things are slower than you'd expect. Even guys like Earl are missing their targets. The sales just aren't where they should be."

I'm not sure what to say. Am I being fired?

Alan sighs again, then leans forward and clasps his hands on the desk. "Mark, I like you. Your father-in-law is a good man. Your wife is a lovely woman. I'd love to keep you on here. You've got great potential—I just need you to show it to me. You with me?"

My hands unclench. I nod earnestly, as if he's just told me some profound secret of the ages. I'm not being fired. But that was definitely a warning shot.

"That's great." He opens and closes his mouth again, as if debating something. "Look," he finally says. "I'm pretty easy-going. What you do with your time is your business." He lowers his voice. "But don't bring it in here, okay? Now go home and sleep it off."

I must be staring blankly because he finally points at my eye. "Go home. Sleep it off, for God's sake."

"I . . ."

"Just go home, Mark."

***

I walk past Jennifer without even looking up. I can feel my cheeks burning.

"Hey," she calls out, "what happened to your eye?"

I let the door shut behind me and head straight for my car before anyone else sees me.

I climb inside and fish for the key in my pocket. Earl and Trevor are still hanging around the service bay. From where I'm parked, they look tiny standing in the shadow of the 60-foot gorilla, and I feel my shame shifting to anger. How the hell am I supposed to sell more cars if those guys can't even do it? Besides, I'm the one that was wearing the stupid monkey suit out in the heat. They're not doing anything.

And it's not like I'm getting any real training at all. My sales education to date is watching Earl hit on women on the lot or seeing Rusty scare them off with stats about horsepower and acceleration.

The warning shot Alan just fired my way is as good as a death sentence. There's no way I'm going to be able to sell anything anytime soon.

I twist the key, pushing the pedal too hard, revving the engine. I see Trevor look over, but I don't care. I'm now faced with the prospect of an angry dinner with Charlotte—one where I'll have to try to explain how it's not my fault that I'm on notice at the job I just got. Or, more accurately, that her father just got me.

I feel my insides clench. Charlotte will, of course, want to help. But "help" will probably mean suggesting I talk to her father.

That, most assuredly, is not going to happen.

I slam the gearshift into reverse and back away from the building. What am I going to do? I have to learn how to sell—that much is certain. No sales means no job. And no job means failure on far too many fronts—at home, at work, with my in-laws. Not to mention the hit to my already-battered self-esteem.

So yes, I need to learn how to sell, and fast. I look over as Earl barks out a laugh and high-fives a mechanic. He looks ridiculous.

No. I'm not going to get help here. I look up at the gorilla waving in the wind. What would old Hank think of that? I wonder. Probably not much. He'd probably have a lot to say about the state of things here, though. Plenty to say, indeed. He'd have us selling cars like hotcakes, I bet.

My foot sits on the brake. My hand falls off the steering wheel and into my lap. I look up at the Langford sign. Then I slowly turn my head to the side.

On the seat beside me is Henry's film canister, "The Last Up."

I look over to the cellar doors and realize that at

this point, I've got nothing to lose.

***

The next three minutes confirm what I've been afraid of all along: I truly am a coward.

The only projector I know of is in the cellar where, as I shudder to recall, the ghost of Henry Langford has possessed a life-sized piece of damp cardboard.

And so I sit in the car, staring first at the film canister in my hands, then at the cellar doors, then back to the film canister.

"Okay, okay. I'll go." I'm not sure who I'm talking to, but saying it aloud seems to help. I finally turn off the engine, step out of the car, and walk to the doors.

Before I can change my mind, I pull one of them open. The cool air and the damp smell swirl around me. I can see the light is still on. I take a deep breath and walk down the stairs.

As I should have expected, it's not scary at all. Henry really is just a damp piece of cardboard, nothing more. His face doesn't change. There's nothing spooky about him at all, and so I ignore his smiling face and dig out the box containing the projector.

It takes me a few minutes to figure out how to feed the film into the machine. There's a series of spools and spring-loaded rollers that threaten to bring my headache back to life, but with some persistence, I get the spools clipped onto the projector's collapsible arms, and the film woven through the maze.

I plug the power cord into a dangerously ancient-looking receptacle on the back wall, and then take a seat on an overturned crate beside the projector. I flip the switch that powers the bulb.

To my surprise, bright light shines from the projector's lens. It still works. I realize I'll have to turn cellar light off if I really want to see anything, so I walk over to the bottom of the stairs and tug the string hanging from the socket.

The cellar falls into shadow, and I make my way back to my upturned box by the glow of the projector.

As an afterthought, I stand Cardboard Henry up beside me, so he faces the concrete wall that I hope is going to make a passable screen.

"Sorry, Hank. No popcorn. And don't get fresh with me." I laugh, but it comes out a little shrill, and I realize: I'm still scared.

God. What's the matter with me?

I shake my head in disgust and reach over and flip the switch to start the film rolling.

***

Flickering numbers begin to count down on the concrete wall, and I flash back to grade school and children chanting. Ten, nine, eight . . .

I can't remember the last time I watched a real film like this.

Seven, six, five, four . . .

I begin to whisper aloud, "Three, two, one . . ." Then the screen goes black, and light, cheerful music warbles from the aging projector speakers.

A title flashes on the screen:

"The Last Up"
Part 1: The Problem with Selling Cars

On-screen, we fade in on a shot of Langford Auto Sales as it used to be. The film is in black and white, and I immediately recognize the picture. It's an image I've seen a thousand times hanging on the wall of the dealership, but with one difference: it's live.

The pennants draped across the lot flutter in the breeze. People mill about the dealership, inspecting the latest models, and traffic rolls by on the street out front.

"Ah, the busy automotive dealership," a narrator says. "Home of happy salesmen and happy customers."

The narrator sounds like the same guy from every cheesy film I sat through as a kid. It has the classic speech cadence of old newsreels, and it warbles with the poor sound of the projector.

"A career in automobile sales can be an exciting and rewarding way to better yourself," he continues.

I chuckle to myself. "Right. So far so good."

"But today's car buyer is an informed customer." The image cuts to the dealership lot. "Just ask our salesman George."

A man with a plaid sports jacket sits with his feet propped up on a desk. He bears a striking resemblance to Earl—every bad stereotype of the car salesman rolled into one.

He is also asleep.

An alarm sounds. On the wall of the dealership, a

large, red bell marked "UP" is ringing madly.

The shot cuts back to George, who jerks upright. He smooths his hair and straightens his plaid jacket.

The shot cuts to the lot, where George swaggers up to a well-dressed couple.

George pats the hood of an aging clunker, then turns and winks at the camera. The woman looks skeptical.

"No tricks for this sharp customer," says the narrator. The husband shakes his head. "He's not buying."

George looks on, clueless, as the couple marches from the lot. He really is like Earl. I'm starting to wish I had popcorn after all.

The film cuts to George, sitting at his desk and looking dejected.

"George has tried everything."

A series of shots of George trying different sales approaches flashes on the screen.

"He's tried playing it cool," says the narrator.

George tries to be aloof. He taps his finger on the price sticker on a windshield, and then leans against the car, arms crossed. A customer looks at him incredulously. George shrugs his shoulders and stares off at some distant point.

"But no dice. How about price cutting, George?"

George replaces the price sticker on the clunker with a lower price. Nothing. Then a lower price. Then lower still. Customer after customer shakes their head no.

"Sorry, George. No deal. Why not try to attract a little more attention?"

I stare in disbelief, and then laugh out loud as a man in a gorilla suit and a plaid jacket—clearly George— runs after another couple as they flee the lot.

I can't believe it. Earl's getting me to do stuff they laughed at half a century ago.

The shot cuts back to George, now sitting at his desk in the gorilla suit, the mask off. He's seriously bummed out. "Looks like George has got himself in some hot water," says the narrator. "He'll be lucky to cover his draw this month."

On-screen, George's head sinks lower and lower until his forehead touches the desk.

"But don't worry, George," says the narrator. "We've got just—"

The sound stops, the screen goes bright white, and there's a flicking sound that I recognize immediately: the film has broken.

Just as I was really starting to enjoy myself.

"Well, Hank," I say out loud, "it looks like I may not get to learn your secrets after all." I turn to take a look at the projector. With the bare bulb shining on the wall, I can see where the film has broken. I can probably just feed it back through and keep watching.

I walk over and tug the string to turn on the cellar lights, then walk back to turn off the projector bulb.

I start to re-feed the celluloid strip, but my fingers are unsteady. There's something nagging at me. I don't know what it is, but I feel uneasy. I shrug it off and start to feed the film a little faster.

The feeling of uneasiness builds, and my fingers start to sweat. My breathing speeds up. What the hell is wrong with me?

Then it hits me.

I spin around.

Henry Langford is gone.

Where there once was a damp, man-shaped cardboard cutout in coaching gear, there's now . . . nothing. He's just vanished. It's like he got up and walked away.

Every hair on my body stands on end.

I step slowly away from the projector, backing out

into the empty space. I look to the ground, hoping to see that his cardboard body has simply slipped unnoticed to the floor. I know, though, that he's not there. I know it with a certainty. Henry Langford isn't on the floor because—

The lights in the cellar go out almost at the same time the projector comes to life; the light blinds me, and the reels spin wildly. I back up against the wall, and then everything goes black.

***

I wake up, my head resting on my arms.

A dream, I think. But before I can even get my bearings, a whistle shrieks in my ear and I jerk upright. A voice yells, "Cut!"

I'm behind my desk. I can see the cars on the lot and the cars on the showroom floor. Traffic drifts by in the distance.

I'm at work. I'm at the dealership. Langford Auto. I'm where I'm supposed to be.

But I don't think I'm *when* I'm supposed to be.

There's not a car in sight newer than the 1950s. Everything I see is a classic. Some good, some bad—but all classics. It's like I've woken up in a museum.

"That's a wrap, everyone."

The voice comes from a man sitting in a director's chair across the showroom floor from me. Another man fusses with a camera on a tripod, while two others begin taking down sets of portable lights.

"That's it for today, everyone," the director says. Then he looks over at me. "You. Follow me."

That's when I realize the man is Henry Langford. In the flesh.

My mouth falls open, and I stare at him. It's actually him. He's in his coach's outfit. The silver whistle sits in the corner of his mouth.

This is a dream.

That's the only explanation. I'm asleep. I'm in bed at home with Charlotte, and this whole thing is a dream.

"Well, come on," Dream Henry says. "You're here about the job. So let's talk."

The second I realize I'm dreaming, I feel the stress drain out of my body, and I almost laugh out loud.

And since I'm dreaming, I get up and follow a dead man out the front door of a 1950s car dealership like it's the most natural thing in the world.

CHAPTER 4

FIRST GEAR

From behind, Henry looks slightly taller than his cardboard twin, but still a bit shorter than I had imagined. I have a feeling that all the stories have made him seem like a giant in my mind. Size aside, the man has a confidence about him that's undeniable, and he strolls the lot like a king surveying his domain.

My head spins as I try to take in the inventory of vehicles. I've never seen any of these cars up close before, and I've certainly never seen them new. If Langford Auto had these cars on the lot right now, we'd be the richest auction house on the planet.

I briefly wonder how my sleeping brain is able to

create such fantastic detail for things I've never actually encountered, but Henry interrupts me.

"First thing you need to know is this," he says. He pulls out a pack of cigarettes and lights one. He takes a drag and points it at my hand. "We don't go for any of this."

I follow his finger down and realize I'm still clutching the gorilla mask. In fact, I'm wearing the whole suit. When did that happen?

"You work here, there are rules," he continues. "First, you start by knocking off the monkey business."

I hold the mask behind my back.

"Customers aren't rubes at a county fair," Henry continues. "We're not selling snake oil." He spreads his arms wide. "Look around, kid. Look at the streets. We're selling the most important product ever built. We treat our customers and our cars with what they deserve—respect."

He turns to look at me.

"Sure," I say. It's a dream, right? I may as well agree.

"Next, there's a week's training. No commission on any sales."

Before I can say anything, he raises a hand. "Don't even try. I've got guys lining up for this job. I'll give you credit—volunteering for the monkey part in the film was a smart way to get to the front of the line. But it ain't getting you any favors, kid. You do the week of training like everyone else."

I shrug. Why not?

Henry folds his arms across his chest. "Look, kid. I know it sounds like a week of doing something for nothing, but I'm telling you different. You want to learn how to sell cars? How to sell anything? You spend a week with me, and you'll know how."

Henry has been staring at me intensely, but his gaze suddenly refocuses behind me. I turn to see what he's looking at. It takes a moment, but I realize he's not looking at anything in particular. Just staring across the lot.

I turn back to him and wait in silence.

"Sheer beauty, kid. Sheer beauty."

He begins to walk away from me, still gazing across the lot. His hand trails gently across the hood of the nearest sedan.

This, I realize, is a man who absolutely loves what he does. I look across the lot of gleaming cars. Maybe a week with Henry Langford is exactly what I need.

Except, of course, for the fact that I'm dreaming.

But ... so what if I am? Who says you can't learn something from dreams?

"When can I start?" I call after him.

"You already did. Now get that suit off," he calls back, without looking at me.

I scramble after him, trying to catch up and get the monkey suit off at the same time. I feel a strange tingling in my stomach, and it occurs to me that I'm actually excited about going to work.

And for a few moments, I completely forget that I'm dreaming.

***

After a quick tour of the lot, we make our way back inside. Henry hands me a cup of coffee and points at the chair beside his desk, which is right out on the sales floor like everyone else's.

I sit.

"Okay, kid. Tell me why you're here."

Because I'm dreaming?

"To learn how to sell cars," I finally say.

"Then we've got ourselves our first problem."

I stare at him in confusion. "But I thought—"

"That's today's lesson, kid. You want to learn to sell? Then your first job is to stop selling."

I stare at him. "You're telling me that as a salesman, my job is to stop selling?"

"Yep." Henry leans back in his chair, a smug expression on his face. I get the sense he's enjoying this—and has enjoyed it many times before. He watches me for a moment longer, then he says, "Tell me what selling is."

I think for a moment. "Selling is convincing people to buy."

"Wrong. That's exactly wrong. It's exactly why I'm telling you to stop selling."

"I don't understand."

Henry opens a drawer in his desk and pulls out a tube of paper. He unrolls it, then flips it around and spreads it out on the desk so it faces me.

It's a large map of the city and surrounding area. Henry sets his coffee cup on one end to anchor the map, and I do the same on my end.

There's an X on the spot I recognize as the home of Langford Auto. The city itself, though, is a fraction of the size it will be in fifty years.

"See this?" Henry waves his hand around the outside of the city. "All farmland when I grew up. But that's changing now. They're putting houses out there now—way out. Making the roads bigger. And the President just announced that big interstate program. Soon, all the cities will be connected."

I think back to the photo of Henry and Eisenhower hanging in the dealership. No dummy, our Hank.

"All of that means one thing, kid. Everyone needs a car. In fact, I think a lot of 'em are going to need two."

"Doesn't that mean we should be convincing them to buy ours?"

"You're missing the point, kid. You don't need to convince them. They already want to buy."

He lifts his cup, and the map rolls across the desk.

"When they walk onto this lot, they already want and need a car. You don't need to do any selling."

"Then why am I even here? Why not put a tin can out there and let people put their money in and drive off?"

Henry looks at me carefully, and for a moment it seems like he might actually be considering the idea. Then his eyes light up, and he bursts out laughing.

"You're a real card, kid. A real card." He laughs even harder, and I look around to see if anyone is watching, but the dealership is empty.

"As much as I would love not having to pay salesmen," Henry says, regaining his composure, "this place wouldn't last without them. Guys like you are what make everything work."

I roll that around in my mind. "So . . . salespeople

make everything work, but they don't sell?"

Henry leans forward on the desk. "I've seen every kinda salesman, kid," he says. "The big talkers with the boots. The shy ones. The piston heads. The cheerful ones and the miserable S-O-Bs. The ones that never shut up and the ones that never say anything."

I think back to Rusty at the dealership. A piston head for sure. Trevor is the shy one. And Earl? Well . . . he's mostly a miserable S-O-B with big boots.

"They all have one thing in common," Henry continues. "They don't sell as many cars as they should. They don't reach their full potential. You know why?"

"Because . . . no one taught them?" I finally venture.

Henry eyes me suspiciously. "Yeah. That's right. But don't be kissing my behind. What is it that no one taught them?"

"How to sell?" As soon as the words leave my mouth, I try to take them back. "No, wait! I don't know..." I trail off.

Henry sighs. "Kid, nobody taught these characters how to sell cars without selling."

"So if salespeople aren't supposed to sell, what are we supposed to do?"

Henry squints at me. "Why do you keep calling them that?"

"What?"

"Salespeople? They teach you that word in college or something? I'll tell you right now, folks don't like being talked down to. They're not gonna like you as a salesperson any more than a salesman."

With that, he stands up and brushes past me. Political correctness, I realize, is a few decades away.

I follow him across the floor and into the room that will one day be his son's office. For now, I can see it's serving as a small makeshift theater. There's a row of desks, a screen on the wall, and a projector. *The* projector, I realize.

"Grab a seat," Henry says. He begins to fiddle with the projector. "I've got big plans. Taking Langford Auto across the nation. Going to teach every salesman to sell without selling. That's why I'm making these films. Think of them as Henry Langford in a can." He chuckles to himself and then stands up from behind the projector. "And you're going to be my first test-subject."

A wave of uncertainty washes over me. Wasn't I just watching this projector before I arrived . . . *here?*

"Listen carefully. You need to learn five things from me. That's what these pictures are about. They're not finished yet, but I'll let you have a sneak peek right now."

He nods toward a switch on the wall, and I flip the lights off.

"Remember. Five things. You learn them all, and I guarantee you'll make a fortune in this business—and love every minute of it."

He lets the words sink in.

Dreaming or not, Henry Langford has got my attention.

Henry turns the projector on. "Now, pay attention," he says, "and you'll get the answer to your question, Mr. Smarty College Salesperson."

The screen lights up, and the same countdown I saw in the cellar appears. The cheesy music I'd heard before lurches back to life, along with the voice of the 1950s narrator.

The same opening sequence begins—the Langford lot; George, the failed sales rep; the monkey suit—and runs right through to poor George hanging his head over his desk.

Once again, I'm fully drawn into the film's unspoken promise of a better way to sell cars when the screen flickers and then washes out to the bright, blinding light of a white screen.

I hear the tick, tick, tick as the celluloid tail of the

film spins on the rear spool. The film has broken again. Frustrated, I turn to face Henry.

"You want the lights back on to fix—"

My heart lurches in my chest. Henry, the man, is gone. In his place is a slightly damp, slightly bent cardboard cutout. A shadow of the man himself. Henry the cardboard coach.

I feel the edges of the cardboard boxes I'm sitting on and smell the damp of the cellar. I'm back at Langford. The Langford of now, that is.

And I'm faced with something I've suspected all along: this is no dream.

***

I pass the next morning in a sort of delusional half-awareness. The lot is quiet, which isn't great, but I'm not sure how well I would have fared trying to deal with a customer anyway.

Fortunately, Earl isn't around either, and I'm left to try to make sense of what's happened. Right now, I'm faced with two possibilities. The first is that yesterday I traveled back in time to the 1950s and spent the afternoon with the founder of the dealership I work at now. A man, I should add, who's been dead for decades.

The second option is that I've completely lost it.

Neither seems like a road I want to go down, and rather than focus on the fact that I might be going insane, I turn my attention to the reality that I'm insanely thirsty. My adventure in the gorilla suit must have dehydrated me more than I thought. I make a mental note to keep a water bottle close at hand today.

When I'm not busy trying to decide if I'm nuts, my mind keeps wandering back to Henry's claim.

Five things. You learn them all, and I guarantee you'll make a fortune in this business—and love every minute of it.

That's a compelling pitch. But maybe that's all it is. Maybe I'm just being sold. But why would he sell me? After all, that was his whole idea—that sales isn't about selling.

But how can sales not be about selling? The idea doesn't make sense . . . yet . . . it does. It explains a few things. Why people avoid us on the lot like the plague. Why they look at me so warily when I approach them. Don't I do the same thing when salespeople approach me? No thanks, just looking. How many times have I said it myself?

But just when I think that what Henry is saying

makes real sense, some other part of my brain kicks in and reminds me that Henry isn't saying anything.

Henry's been dead for years.

Time travel isn't possible.

Ghosts aren't real.

And yet, I'm sure I'm not dreaming. I've pinched myself. I've walked around. I've snuck out to my car to try to fall asleep, thinking that if I woke up again in my dream, I'd wake up for real. I've even searched online for tips on how to wake up from a dream.

If I can search online for tips on how to wake up, surely I must really be awake. Right? And if I'm awake, that leaves just two options—either I'm crazy or what happened actually happened.

This endless argument is looping through my brain for the thousandth time when I become aware that someone is standing at my desk. It's Trevor. How long has he been standing there? If it were Earl, I wouldn't have to wonder because he would have been in my face all along, but with Trevor, it's hard to tell. He could have been there for fifteen minutes.

"What's up, Trevor?"

He's doing his Trevor thing, kind of looking down and off to the side, like there's something on the floor that I really should be picking up. I worked here a full week before I stopped looking behind me trying to figure out what he was staring at. Now, I know: he's not looking at anything; he's just trying to look anywhere but at me.

"Nothing. Pretty quiet today." His eyes flicker somewhere around my shirt pocket. Not exactly eye contact, but pretty good for Trevor.

"Well, I think the next up is yours. Maybe today is your lucky day," I say.

Trevor laughs a little. Actually, it's more of a self-deprecating snort that says, *when hell freezes over.* "You can have mine if you want," he says glumly. "It's not like I'm going to close anyone."

He says the word "close" like he's trying to sound out a word in a new language. It's something foreign that he can't quite wrap his tongue around.

All the while, his eyes flit from my shirt to my desk, from my desk to the floor behind me, and then back to my shirt again.

I'm no sales genius, but I can't fathom how Trevor could possibly sell a car.

As soon as the thought flashes through my mind, Henry's words are ringing in my ears again.

Stop selling.

Trevor barely talks to ups on the lot. He says it's

because he can't—that he wasn't built that way—but what if it's not true? If Henry can train people across the country, then surely Trevor can learn.

Trevor, I realize, isn't just shy. It's not about that. The problem is that he doesn't want to be a "closer" or "land a big fish." It's in his language, his posture, his attitude—he doesn't want to sell people.

But he doesn't have to. Right? Isn't that what Henry was telling me? Trevor doesn't want to sell, but if old Hank is right, then Trevor doesn't need to.

The door chimes.

In my mind, an alarm bell that reads "UP" on it starts ringing. A man approaches reception. I can hear Jennifer say, "Just one minute. I'll have one of our sales advisors help you out." Jennifer looks over to Trevor and me and discreetly nods her head toward the man.

I look over at Trevor, who's suddenly been stricken deaf, blind, and dumb.

I should just take the up, I tell myself. It wouldn't be stealing—after all, Trevor told me I could. God knows I could use the sale. But it's really Trevor's. We're a team, right?

The thought brings a new image to mind: Henry Langford in his coaching outfit.

"Be right there, sir," I call over to the man. He waves

casually in acknowledgment and wanders into the main showroom area to check out the floor models.

"Trevor," I say quietly, "this one's yours."

"You take him, Mark," he says. "Maybe you'll have better luck than me. I'm just not a salesman."

In my mind, I hear the shriek of Henry Langford's whistle. It's so real I almost jump.

"Trevor, do you trust me?"

His eyes flit up, almost reaching my face. "Huh?"

"Do you trust me?"

"Sure, Mark."

"Then just do what I tell you. I want you to go over to that guy."

"What's the point? I told you, I'm just not a salesman."

"Then don't sell."

Trevor chuckles nervously. "Thanks for the great advice, Mark."

"I'm serious. Go over there and say anything you want to that guy—anything at all, you hear me? Just follow this one rule: you may not sell him a car."

"Mark—"

"I'm serious. Do whatever you want. It's your up. But no selling. None. Understand?"

"You're serious?"

"Deadly."

Trevor looks across the sales floor at the man.

"Go."

"Alright," he says, then stands and starts to make his way to the floor.

"Trevor," I call after him.

He turns to look at me.

"Relax," I say. "It's not like you're going to sell any less, right?"

A smile crosses his face.

"Just go over there and don't sell."

He takes one more look at me, as if he's checking to see if this is some kind of joke, then shakes his head in wonder and crosses the floor.

***

A full hour later—really, a full hour—Trevor finds his way back to my desk. I tried to eavesdrop on his conversation with the customer, but after a few minutes, the two of them headed out to the lot.

Regardless of what happened out there, though, this has to be a record for Trevor. He's so damn shy that a normal conversation on the sales floor for Trevor is minutes at most. In the time it takes me to pour and stir a cup of coffee and walk back to my desk, any up that Trevor's been talking to is usually long gone.

This time is different, though, and Trevor's face shows it. He's still looking at some imaginary focal point behind my left armpit, but he's smiling. A little.

"Hey," I say, standing up, "how was that?"

"Good," he says. "I did just what you said, and I think it really worked." There's a new energy in his voice.

"So . . . what happened? Where is he? Test drive?"

"Gone home, I think."

A very faint alarm bell starts to ring in my mind.

"And he's coming back?"

He shrugs. "Beats me. Nice guy though. I have to thank you, Mark. Your idea really helped. Who taught you that?"

Oh, some dead guy. You've probably heard of him— Henry Langford?

I probe a little further. "So . . . you're going to call him?"

He shrugs again. "I'll wait for him to call, I guess. I don't have his number or anything."

"Trevor, you talked to the guy for an hour. You didn't get his contact info?"

His head jerks back a little, like I've just put an idea

in his brain that's so new the sheer weight of it has pitched him off balance.

"I just never thought of it, Mark. You told me not to sell, so I just talked to the guy. I didn't do one bit of selling. It was great, really. I'm almost looking forward to the next one."

And with that, he saunters off toward the coffee-maker, blissfully unaware that he just blew a potential sale—probably his first real chance in weeks.

I shake my head at poor Trevor. The guy is hopeless.

I turn back to my paperwork, but the whole situation begins to nag at me. Trevor didn't sell, that's for sure. He did just what Henry told me, and what I told him.

But what did he do instead? As near as I can tell, nothing more than make conversation. For all I know, they just talked baseball the whole time. Now I'm starting to feel like it's my fault. If it weren't for me, Trevor might have actually sold a damn car to the guy, but I went and got in the way. I should have kept my mouth shut.

And yet everything Henry told me has a ring of truth to it. It just feels right. People don't want to be sold. And guys like Trevor don't want to sell. It all makes sense.

But what should I have told Trevor to do instead?

The thought continues to grow in my mind. I'm getting nothing done. My legs are jittery, and when I notice Jennifer looking over at me from the reception desk, I realize I've been tapping my pen on my coffee mug.

I stop and shrug. "Sorry."

"Forget it," she says. "It's quitting time anyway. You want me to lock up behind you?"

I look around and realize everyone's gone. When did that happen? Probably when I was busy trying to figure out exactly what Coach Langford didn't tell me during our time together because we were interrupted.

Interrupted, I recall, by the film breaking...

"That's okay," I say. "I've got something I need to finish up."

***

After Jennifer drives off the lot, I lock up and head around the side of the building to the storm cellar doors.

It's still blistering hot out, and the thirst hits me again. Why didn't I bring a water bottle?

My heart jumps a bit as I lift open the heavy doors and step into the cool gloom of the cellar. This place is still giving me the creeps.

Cardboard Henry is right where I left him, but I'm not wasting any time on him right now. I'm a man on a mission. Either the cellar of Langford Auto is a time portal to the 1950s . . . or it isn't. It's that simple, and I intend to find out the truth right now. In the process, I'll also find out if I'm nuts. So all in all, I'm feeling like it's a good plan.

I feed the broken film through the projector again and put my hand on the switch. I take a deep breath and turn the projector on.

The screen comes to life, briefly, as the film resumes. Then everything flashes to white as the celluloid runs back out through the reels, and pure, bright light washes over the room.

***

I'm prepared this time. I notice as the sensation of the crate I'm sitting on fades away, almost as if I've floated off the box. There's a brief sense of weightlessness, then a gradual increase in pressure beneath me. I'm sitting again. I'm behind a desk. I can feel the wood under my elbows, the seat underneath me.

Before I can even open my eyes to get my bearings, I'm nearly startled out of my chair by an incredibly loud, shrill, whistle. Again.

I'm back in the showroom at Langford. The 1950's Langford. It's official—I've actually traveled through time.

I'm not alone. The showroom has more than a dozen other people in it. Some stand, while others sit at desks like me or perch on tables. In the center of the showroom, next to an enormous winged sedan, stands Henry Langford. He looks like a pristine reincarnation of the aging cardboard cutout—the coach in all his glory before years of water damage and deterioration. In his mouth is the silver whistle, the lanyard looping around his neck.

"That's all, people," Henry says. "That was a good day. Let's have another tomorrow."

With that, the group begins to disperse. The men all don hats as they leave, holding the door for the women. I try not to catch anyone's eye, but it doesn't seem like anyone is really noticing me. I wait until the last employee leaves, then walk over to where Henry has taken a seat at his desk. I pause a moment, then clear my throat.

"Hey, kid," Henry says without looking up. "How'd it go today?"

What do you say in the 1950s? Swell?

"Fine," I tell him instead.

Henry flips a page on his desk. "Fine? Doesn't look like you sold anything." He leans back and looks me over.

I smile. "Well . . . you told me not to sell." I laugh, but it dies in my chest as I realize he's not seeing the humor. I feel my throat tighten, and my already-parched mouth goes drier still.

"Could I have a bottle of water?"

Henry looks at me. "A bottle of water?"

I keep forgetting where I am. Or, rather, *when* I am. "Never mind."

Henry shakes his head and continues. "I told you not to sell," he affirms. "But what did I tell you to do instead?"

I think back to my last visit with Henry. The film broke before he could tell me. Or I was sent back to the future. Or something. Regardless, Henry never told me what to do instead of selling.

And truthfully, I didn't do any selling that day anyway. I passed on my only shot at an up when Trevor offered me his, and he did a whole lot of 'not selling' for me.

So what did he do?

"I guess I just made conversation," I say finally.

Henry considers this. "Okay. Conversation isn't bad. But conversation is just talking without a purpose. We don't do that here."

I drop into the seat in front of Henry's desk. "Okay. So I don't sell, and I don't make conversation. What should I be doing?"

Henry eyes me. "You remember I said you had to learn five things from me?"

"Sure." I'm wondering how I'm going to learn two never mind five if I can't even get past the first one, but I keep that thought to myself.

"Each of those five things isn't just about knowing something, kid. It's about doing something. It's about making a change. A shift—like changing gears."

Changing gears. Okay, car talk. This, I can do.

"So what's the first shift?"

"When you try to sell someone, you're shifting into reverse. You're not moving things forward. You're actually moving them backward—away from the sale."

He's right. The whole game of "sales" as far as I can see, tends to push people away more often than bring them in. I wonder if guys like Trevor know this intuitively. Maybe they're smarter than the rest of us. Maybe they already know that selling just doesn't work.

"So how do I get into first gear? What's the first shift?"

Henry leans forward, energized. "Okay. Let me make this simple for you. You ever buy a tomato?"

"Sure."

"And what did the salesman tell you the last time you bought tomatoes?"

"Uh—"

"Exactly," Henry cuts in. "You don't need a salesman to buy and sell tomatoes. You just go buy a tomato. It's easy. There's nothing between you and the tomato, except maybe the grocer. But he's just making change."

"But cars aren't tomatoes."

"Exactly." Henry leans back in his chair, satisfied.

I stare at him blankly.

He sighs and leans forward again. "Okay kid. How come people don't just walk up to the counter here and put down a stack of bills and drive away in a new car? We do it for tomatoes, why not cars?"

I'm completely confused.

"I don't know. Cars are . . . different."

"Sure they are. Cars are harder to buy. But why? I'll tell you, Mr. College Graduate. In between wanting a car and getting a car is something that everyone has—a problem."

I'm about to ask what that problem is, but Henry doesn't give me a chance.

"That problem could be anything. Money. Uncertainty. Not sure what car is best. Fear of making the wrong decision. Getting buy-in from the wife."

Did he just say "the wife"?

"It could be getting a loan or wondering how to get rid of the old jalopy they came in with," Henry continues. "Regardless, the story is the same. Every up has a problem. If all they wanted was a car, they'd have bought one already. And since they're standing on our lot, it means one thing and one thing only: they have a problem. If they don't, then we can go right back to your idea of leaving a tin can out for people to put their money in. They can drive away in their tomato without any help from us."

It's all beginning to make perfect sense.

"So that means your job," he announces, "is to—"

"—to solve their problem," I finish.

"Exactly," Henry says, then grins. "There's hope for

you yet, kid."

We sit in silence for a moment while I roll this idea around. It's hard to argue with the logic. If buying a car were easy, people would just ... buy them. Like tomatoes. But they don't do that. And that means buying cars must be hard for the buyer.

Henry is right. Buyers have a problem.

"So my goal is to solve their problems," I say.

"That's exactly right. The first shift—the first gear, if you like—is about changing your goal. It's about shifting from selling to solving. Do that, and you'll start to move things forward."

"No more sales," I say.

"No more sales," Henry repeats. "A sale is just a transaction. You give me money; I give you a tomato. A sale isn't something we do to people, kid. A sale is what happens after we help solve someone's problem."

Henry leans back in his chair and crosses his arms triumphantly. He's clearly said this more than once. More than a thousand times, I bet.

After a moment, he leans forward again. "Know what that means?"

I shake my head. As long as it doesn't mean blowing the damn whistle, I'm good.

"It means you get a new job title. You can't be a

salesman anymore."

"So I'm a . . . solvesman?"

Henry grunts. "At least you didn't say solvesper-son. But that isn't it, and I'll tell you why. First of all, it sounds stupid. Second, it doesn't quite cover the bases. There's more to it."

"So what do I call myself?"

Henry gets a sly glint in his eye. "I'm not telling you yet. But I can tell you this. 'Up' doesn't just mean another shot at a sale."

"Then what does it mean?"

"It means 'unidentified problem.' In fact, kid, you've taken your last up. From now on, if you follow my advice, you'll see every customer as a problem that needs to be identified—and then solved."

Henry is clearly pleased with himself.

My thirst returns. "Can I get a . . . glass of water."

Henry eyes me suspiciously. "Why are you so thirsty, kid? It sure ain't from selling cars."

Because I was nearly killed in a gorilla suit and then suffered a concussion, which led me to discover time travel?

"I . . . I was out jogging earlier."

"Jogging?" He looks at me blankly.

Of course. No one jogs in the 1950s.

"My memory," I say, scrambling. "It needs . . . jogging. I guess that's why I didn't quite get all you were saying yesterday."

He seems to buy it.

"So what's the second shift?" I ask, desperate to change the subject.

He seems pleased by my interest, but glances at his watch.

"Well, kid. We all need a little extra coaching now and then. What do you say we kill two birds with one stone? We'll go to Ray's, take care of your thirst, and shift you into second gear while we're at it."

FIRST GEAR

The Shift: From Selling to Solving

Between every customer and every sale is a problem. Your job is to identify the problem and solve it.

CHAPTER 5

SECOND GEAR

The walk from Langford Auto is perhaps the most surreal experience of my life.

Not only is the front lot of the dealership a veritable museum of classic cars, but the whole town is. I keep waiting for someone to yell, "Cut!" and reveal that the whole thing is just a movie set. But a part of me knows that's not going to happen. It feels too real.

After strolling across the Langford lot, we cross under the lines of waving pennants that front the road and stand on the sidewalk. A few decades from now, a guy in a gorilla suit is going to be standing on this same spot wondering if the best parts of his life have already passed him by.

So far, I've been doing pretty well at handling all this. But it's that thought—that my future self will be standing right here, in this very spot—that finally blows my mind. I need a drink. And this time it's not because I'm thirsty.

Whoever Ray is, I hope he runs a bar.

We cross the street and head downtown. The street names are familiar, and I recognize some of the older buildings by their architecture, but there isn't a single store with the same name . . . with the exception of Langford Auto.

The movie theatre is still in the same place, but it's playing *The Bridge On The River Kwai*. The sidewalks are surprisingly full of pedestrians. Even though the city is many times bigger in my time, it feels like there are more people walking around it in the 1950's. And every one of them seems to know Henry Langford.

"Afternoon, Mr. Langford."

"Hey, Hank."

"Hello, Henry."

Henry clearly enjoys this and has a smile for everyone. But he's also a man on a mission, and he never stops walking. My head swivels as I pass an hon-est-to-goodness barber pole. Inside the shop, a man sits in the chair getting an old-fashioned shave, while another waits reading the newspaper. I slow and squint at the newsprint through the glass.

It's August 29, 1957.

It's the same day on the calendar as it was when I woke up this morning. But it's a completely dif-ferent year.

I'm really here.

Everything seems to be moving in slow motion. The classic cars passing on the street. The men in Fedoras. The butcher shop. The bakery. The women pushing prams. Kids in aprons carrying paper grocery bags.

I'm really here. I'm in 1957. Even my parents are here somewhere, I realize ... only they haven't even met each other yet.

And I haven't been born.

The whole idea is making my head hurt all over again.

"You coming, kid?"

Henry's voice breaks my trance, and I see he's stopped in front of the next door. "Let's get that thirst taken care of."

He holds the door open for me, and I step inside.

***

Ray doesn't run a bar. But my disappointment is quickly replaced by amazement. As I look at the sign on the wall, I realize I'm getting my first look at a real "Soda Shop."

If this whole thing is a scene from a movie, then this is the most detailed movie set ever made. It's also one of the busiest. This place is packed.

Black and white tiles checkerboard across the floor, then disappear from view under the booths that run around the perimeter of the shop. A jukebox in the corner plays an old Elvis tune.

No. It's a new Elvis tune, I realize.

People are dancing, talking, laughing. The booths are crammed with teenagers. A harried waitress carries an enormous tray of burgers, fries, and drinks in tall soda glasses.

Directly in front of me is a long, shining counter fronted by bar stools on gleaming metal poles. Behind the counter is a man dressed in white. He wears a simple white cap on his salt-and-pepper head. In his hand he holds a cloth that's moving over the chrome surfaces of the soda fountains in front of him. They're already gleaming, but his hand keeps moving in a fluid, practiced motion.

Despite the mayhem around him, though, his attention is focused solely on the words being spoken by the person in front of him—an earnest-looking teenaged girl in a poodle skirt and loose sweater.

I follow Henry to the counter where two empty stools remain.

As we sit, the girl hops down, and her tight ponytail bounces behind her. "Thanks so much, Mr. Weathers," she says over the noise. "I knew you'd know what to do." She smiles, then turns and picks her way through the crowd toward the door.

The man in white turns his attention to us. "Hank, it's great to see you." He moves his cloth to his other hand and sticks out a palm in my direction. "Hello, son. Ray Weathers. Pleasure to meet you. Don't mind the craziness. After-school crowd."

I shake his hand. "Mark Dunham."

"My friend here," says Henry, patting me on the

back, "seems to have an unquenchable thirst."

"That so?" says Ray. "What have you tried so far?"

"I . . . I drank some water."

"How'd that work for you?"

I clear my throat, which feels like sandpaper. "I'm still pretty parched, to be honest." The truth is I'm dying for more water. I can't seem to get enough of it.

"You always this thirsty?"

"No. Just today, I guess."

"Just today, huh?" Ray seems to be deep in thought, but his cloth keeps moving in circles on the counter, then over the chrome of the soda fountain.

A chorus of laughter erupts nearby. Ray seems not to notice.

"What happened yesterday?" he asks after a moment.

I'm not sure how to reply. I nearly died of dehydration, suffered a concussion, and traveled through time. You?

"I think maybe I didn't drink enough," I say instead.

"Working outside, were you?"

"Um . . . yes."

"Well. This has been some crazy weather. Record heat wave, I hear. I'd say your system is out of balance. When that happens you can drink all the water you want but never get your fill. You need to rebalance. I've got just the thing for you."

I look at Henry.

"Go ahead. It's on me, kid."

Ray busies himself behind the counter. He mixes a whole series of ingredients together, then blends the works with a gleaming silver appliance. Moments later, he hands the concoction to me in a tall soda glass with a straw.

"Try that," he says with a smile.

I take a few sips. Then a few more. It's delicious, and I drain half the glass in less than a minute.

My thirst vanishes. Just like that.

Ray sees the look on my face and smiles. "I think we solved your problem."

Henry orders a float, and I take a few more sips of Ray's magic elixir.

"That the Henderson girl who just left?" Henry asks.

"Yes, sir. She had a problem. Boy trouble, I guess you might say."

"She looked happy enough when she left," I note. "Couldn't have been that much of a problem."

Henry grins. "Everyone leaves here smiling, kid. That's why Ray's still in business, and every other soda shop in town goes under in six months."

I look around. Ray is more than just in business. The place is jammed.

"Well, if you make something this good for everyone, I can see why." I take a loud slurp from my glass.

Henry chuckles. "Ray pulls a good soda, that's true. But really, how different is one float from the next? No offense, Ray."

"None taken. Any monkey can scoop ice cream."

Interesting choice of words, I think.

We're interrupted by a teenaged boy in a leather jacket. "Mr. Weathers, can I ask you something?"

"Of course, Pete." He turns to us. "Can you gentlemen excuse me for a few moments?"

I turn my attention back to my drink and finish what's left in the bottom of the glass. Now that my thirst is gone, I'm feeling my focus return. I spin my stool to face Henry.

"Okay. I think I understand first gear. I need to shift from trying to sell, to trying to solve problems. But I'm not sure I understand how to do that. How do I find out what their problem is?"

Henry smiles. He's clearly pleased with the question.

"That, kid, is second gear. It's another shift."

"I think I'm ready to hear it."

Henry taps the whistle around his neck. "I'll be the judge of that. Tell me about first gear."

I think for a moment. "First gear is about shifting from selling to solving. It means I have to change my goal from trying to sell someone a car to solving the problem that's stopping them from buying one."

"Couldn't have said it better myself."

"So how do I do that? How do I solve the problem?"

"Well, that depends on what the problem is," Hank counters. "Take Ray, here. He could have just handed you a cherry coke when you walked in the door. It's what half the kids in here are drinking. But your problem wasn't that you wanted something to sip on while you talked to your friends. You had a real thirst. A real problem."

"And Ray figured out what the problem was," I mused.

"Yep. Second gear starts you down the road to finding that out."

"So how do I do that? Whenever I ask people what's keeping them from buying, they always just tell me it's the price."

"Of course they do," Henry says. "It's not true, but that's what they're going to tell you until you shift into the next gear."

"So what's the shift?"

Henry ponders for a moment.

"Let me ask you this. Tell me about the last time you bought something important. Something expensive."

"Like my car?"

"Nope. Doesn't count. You're a car salesman. Pick something else."

Nothing comes to mind at first, but then I start thinking about what I'd bought that was expensive.

"My wife's engagement ring," I say, finally. "That was a big deal."

"Perfect. How'd that go for you?"

The truth is, it was horrible.

"Not so good."

"Why's that?"

"I was so stressed out about it. I was spending more

money than I ever had before. I had no idea what kind of ring she would like. I didn't know whether I was overpaying. And the salesman kept pushing me to buy a bigger ring. He made me feel like if I didn't, she'd think I didn't love her or something. But what I really wanted was something she'd like. She's got a real eye for these things."

"So what did you do?"

"I almost gave in and just bought a big rock. But then I walked away. The next day I went to another store, and I walked out with the perfect ring. I loved it, and I knew Charlotte would too. When I proposed to her, I never worried once about whether I had the right ring."

"So why'd you buy it at the second place?"

I think back. Why did I buy it there? There was a ring just like it in the first store.

"I'm not sure," I tell him.

"Think back," Henry says. "What did the man at the second store say?"

I pictured the store in my mind. The inside. The rows of lighted glass cabinets. The small man behind the counter. I'd said hello. He'd asked how he could help. I said—

"I got it!" I say. "I told him I was looking for an engagement ring, and he said, 'Then let's have a seat before you go any further. I remember shopping for my wife's ring, and it damn near killed me. We don't want you having a heart attack before you even get a chance to propose.'"

It all floods back to me like it was yesterday. Or about fifty years from yesterday, I think.

I look at Henry. "I don't remember exactly what he said after that, but I walked out of there with a ring."

Henry nods his head. "Of course you did."

He turns back to his soda, as if he's just revealed some obvious truth to me—but it's one that I'm clearly not seeing. I look over to Ray for insight, but there's practically a line-up of teenagers waiting to talk to him.

***

After Henry pays for our drinks, we say goodbye to Ray and head outside. The heat is still intense, but my thirst is gone, replaced by curiosity.

Henry turns the conversation back to my ring shopping experience.

"I'm not even sure why I bought the ring there," I tell him. "I never really thought about it."

Henry nods and smiles at people on the sidewalk. He knows everyone.

"That jeweler knew second gear," he says between hellos. "Maybe it came naturally to him, or maybe he learned it. But one thing's for sure—he knew it. No question."

"So, what is it? What's second gear?"

"Here's the thing. You can't solve someone's problem without finding out what it is. But you can't even begin to find out what it is until you change how you view that person. The first shift changes how you see your job—from someone who sells to someone who solves. The second shift changes how you see your customers."

"I'm not sure I understand."

"The problem with salesmen is that they see customers as targets. As marks, or rubes. It's like a game to them, where they try to outdo the customer by selling them instead of helping them."

Henry tips his hat to a woman who's sweeping the sidewalk outside a restaurant. She smiles warmly back.

"As long as you see a customer that way," he continues, "you'll never discover their problem."

"Why not?"

"Because they'll never tell you. As long as you see them as an opposing team, they're going to see you the same way. And then they're never going to tell you anything. They're going to look at the sticker price and walk away. Every time."

"So how should I see them?"

"The same way the second jeweler—and Ray—saw you. As a partner. A teammate. The first jeweler confronted you. He wanted to win the game. But the second one joined your team. He said, 'Hey. I've been there. It's tough. Let's make sure we get this right.'"

I think back to my experience in the two jewelry stores. Henry is exactly right. Again.

"So I need to put myself in their shoes? What if I've never been in their shoes before?"

"You don't have to be the customer. You just need to appreciate that they're making a big decision, and big decisions are stressful. Take your example of buying a ring. You don't need to be married to have a little sympathy for a fellow who's spending a few months of his dough on a special gal."

I find myself nodding along. Henry is making a compelling case.

"To shift into second gear," Henry continues, "you need to shift from confrontation to collaboration. You need to get on the same team as the customer. There's a problem to solve, and you're going to find out what it is—and then solve it, together."

We reach the end of the main street, the T-intersection where Langford Auto marks one end of the downtown core. Henry stops, and we wait for the traffic to clear.

"Changing how you see your customers," Henry tells me, "changes how the customers see you. They'll stop seeing you as an opponent when you stop looking at them as targets."

"And if I make that shift," I say, "customers will tell me their problems?"

Henry laughs. "Not right away, kid. There's more to it than that. But if you don't shift to second gear, they'll *never* tell you."

We cross the road and pass beneath the waving pennants of the dealership. Henry stops and scans the lot.

"So," I say, "what's the next shift? What's third gear?"

Henry gazes over the sea of shining vehicles.

"Not so fast, kid. Let's go watch a little more of that movie."

SECOND GEAR

The Shift: From Confrontation to Collaboration

To discover your customer's problem, join their team.

CHAPTER 6

THIRD GEAR

I wake in a state of exhaustion. I'm not sore like the day before—except for the marks on my face, I seem to have recovered from my fall down the stairs—but I'm mentally spent. It's as if my brain stayed awake all night while my body slept.

I shouldn't be surprised.

I'm positive now that I'm neither dreaming nor crazy. And that means in the last two days, I've nearly died of dehydration, suffered a concussion, and traveled through time to the 1950s to meet my boss's deceased father. It's a lot to digest.

And if those things aren't pushing my brain

hard enough, there's a new thought emerging from the chaos.

I'm learning a whole new way to sell.

Or . . . not sell, as the case may be. Because I'm convinced that Henry is right—customers don't want to be sold. They don't like it, and they don't need it. What they need is someone they trust to solve their problems.

I'm so preoccupied by the idea of solving other people's problems that it takes me far longer than it should to realize that I've got problems of my own. It's only when I finally head downstairs to grab a cup of coffee that I realize Charlotte is still at home. She starts work early, so she always leaves for work before me in the morning.

Not only is she still here, but she's still wearing a bathrobe. For a moment, I think maybe it's Sunday. Could my fall down the stairs have rattled my brain enough for me to mix up the days?

Apparently not. My 'good morning' earns me little more than a grunt from Charlotte, who's watching the news. I pour a cup of coffee and sit down beside her.

"You're not working today?"

"I haven't decided."

A few more minutes pass in silence.

"I should get going," I finally say.

"Fine."

Oh boy.

"Is everything okay?" I venture.

"Where were you last night?" She's still staring dead ahead at the screen.

Damn. How am I going to explain this? By the time Henry brought me to the projector room, and I traveled back to my own time, it was after dark. By the time I finally got home, it was almost midnight, and Charlotte was asleep.

"I had to stay late at work."

She seems to ponder this. "Okay."

"I'm sorry I didn't call."

Another long pause.

She clears her throat. "Did you get paid this week?"

I was hoping she wouldn't ask. "Just my draw."

I can see her jaw clench.

I think of Henry and the first two shifts. "But I'm learning a lot. I think this month will be a lot better."

I barely get the words out before Charlotte abruptly stands and rushes to the bathroom. She emerges a few minutes later looking very pale.

"Are you okay?" I ask.

The answer, as it turns out, is both yes and no.

***

I'm tragically late for work. Still, I'm almost downtown before I realize I've been driving at half the speed limit. I'm leading a long parade of angry traffic as I poke along at a bicycle's pace.

My brain is wrapped up in a whole new kind of fog. Not one caused by concussions or Henry Langford, but by something that makes even time travel seem somewhat trivial by comparison.

I'm going to be a father.

This was not even on my radar. We'd discussed it, of course, but we'd agreed that there was plenty of time, and that we should establish our careers first. (The "our" being in fact "my" career, which is slowly going down in flames—a point Charlotte drove home quite nicely in the past hour.)

But the luxury of time has vanished, and I can't help but wonder if it's vanished for good. Will there be any more lazy Sunday afternoons watching football? Nights out with the guys? Long vacations without a care in the world?

Is life as I know it gone forever?

I'm sure Charlotte must have these same worries, but at the moment, she seems concerned with only one thing: my ability to provide. And so far I've done a poor job of reassuring her.

In fact, I've done a pretty poor job of everything. I'd been desperate to make her feel better this morning, but everything I said just seemed to make things worse.

I can understand her point. She's pregnant, her whole life is about to change, and she's watching her bruised and battered, half-broke car salesman husband fumble his way toward the coffee pot at a time when any self-respecting future father should be at the office slaying water buffalo to bring home to his family.

I look at my scabbed and stubbled face in the rear-view mirror, and shake my head. If there was a time-travel course on being a good husband, I'd have already flunked out—

—a horn blares, and I startle back to reality. I check the mirror and realize I've slowed down again.

I step on the gas and leave the line behind, but the thought stays with me. If there was a time-travel course on being a good husband . . .

Maybe there is.

Couldn't I use Henry's shifts at home? To change how I see my job as a husband? To change how I see Charlotte?

Didn't I just use them, in my head? To understand Charlotte's point of view, and the problem she needs to solve?

If I'd used Henry's shifts this morning instead of arguing my own selfish point of view, would I be driving to work happy instead of scared half to death?

I'm not sure.

But if there is anything certain about this new development in our life, it's that I need to get my act together.

I need to learn to sell—and fast.

This thought begins to push out all others as I creep up Main Street toward the dealership. And it takes center stage as I pass the discount store on the west side and realize that it's the future—no, the past—home of Ray's Soda Shop.

Customers want someone they trust to solve their problems. That's what Henry had preached and what Ray had demonstrated. And, this morning notwithstanding, I think I'm a pretty good problem solver.

But how do I find that "unidentified problem"—that "up"—to begin with?

The question follows me down the street. I keep looking in my rear-view mirror at the discount store—at Ray's. The thought bounces around some more, tapping at the walls of my mind, nagging at me.

What was it Henry said?

He could have just handed you a cherry coke when you walked in the door.

But Ray didn't do that. Instead, he found my problem, just like that.

But how did he do it?

I continue to mull over the question as I pull into the lot. Earl has the early shift today, and I see he's chosen a good morning. He's standing in front of a sporty little two-door talking to a young professional-looking woman.

Mind you, it's Earl, so he's not just standing. He's got one leather boot up on the bumper of the car. I can't quite tell whether he's playing the part of salesman or porn star, but he clearly thinks the two go hand-in-hand.

Henry Langford must be turning over in his grave. Except I'm not sure he's actually in his grave.

Luckily, no one seems to notice I'm late. I'm not at my desk for more than two minutes when the front door slams and Earl strolls past my desk, whistling a cheery tune. Rusty looks up from a parts book.

"Great morning, boys," Earl says. "Great morning indeed."

I'm not sure if it's his attitude or if I'm overwhelmed by everything that's happened in the last two days, but I can't take it anymore. Maybe it's just the disgust I felt watching Earl on the lot. I don't know what it is, but before I can stop my mouth from opening, I speak up.

"Did she run off before or after you called her little lady?" I ask.

Earl stops in his tracks. "What?"

"I know you lost that up. What scared her off?"

I can almost feel how wide Rusty's eyes are growing.

Earl snorts. "Jealous, college boy? You wish. She's coming back with a check this afternoon." He turns and walks off in triumph.

"No she isn't," I say, loud enough for him to hear.

Earl stops again. "What did you say?"

"She's not coming back. You're lying."

From the corner of my eye, I see Jennifer pick up the phone.

"You scared her off," I continue. "You tried to sell her, just like you try to sell everyone, and you crashed and burned."

Earl's face is turning a deep red, but I can't seem to stop myself. "Why don't you just admit it? You're trying to teach us how to sell, but you don't even know how to do it yourself."

Earl's eyes narrow. I can feel the anger coming off him in waves. He walks right up to me and lowers his voice so it's barely audible.

"You listen to me, you piece of highbrow garbage—"

"Mark."

Alan's voice interrupts from behind just as I think Earl is going to grab me. My heart sinks.

"Could I see you in my office, please?" His voice is very slow, very even. Very you're-about-to-get-fired.

My heart shudders. I can't lose this job. Not today. I just can't.

Earl can see the fear in my eyes. A faint smirk touches the corner of his mouth, and he turns and heads to his desk.

Alan stands aside and lets me walk in first. I can feel the adrenaline from my confrontation with Earl leaving my body the moment I step inside his office.

He follows me in and closes the door.

Baiting Earl like that was stupid. It's only been sixty seconds, but I've already calmed down enough to know what my outburst was about: Earl making me wear the gorilla suit. I wanted to get back at him, but all I really did was make an enemy.

Alan is facing the far wall. His head is bowed.

"Look, I'm really sorr—"

Alan raises his hand to silence me. Then he turns around.

"What are you doing, Mark?" He walks behind his desk. "We both know the guy's an ass. Okay? It's no secret. But he actually does sell cars. Sure, he rubs some people the wrong way. But I need him right now. And what I don't need is you pissing him off."

I feel my cheeks turning pink. "I was just trying to help. I'm sorry. It's just that . . . I don't know. I just think there might be a better way to sell cars."

"And you thought you were that guy?"

"I—"

"You thought that you, the guy who hasn't sold a single car, were the guy to tell my number one salesman how to sell?"

"I—"

"Let me tell you what you should be thinking: start

selling cars or start looking for another job."

My heart is pounding in my chest. This couldn't be happening at a worse time. I open my mouth but nothing comes out.

Alan flops into his chair. He looks at me, shakes his head, and sighs. Then, to my surprise, he breaks into a smile. It's weak, but it's there.

"A better way to sell cars? You sound exactly like my old man. He used to say things like that all the time when I was a kid." Alan is staring into space.

"Maybe . . . he was right," I venture.

He frowns at me. "Don't push your luck, Mark."

I should shut up right now.

But what does that get me? Going back to sales training á la Earl is not going to get me anywhere. It's not going to help me sell. It's not going to feed my family.

I look up at the portrait of Henry standing in front of the Packard with his arms spread, grinning at the camera. "He did pretty well, right? Your dad?"

Alan shakes his head, ruefully. "Cars were his life, that's for sure." He looks up at the photo. "And the end of it too. Did you know my father died in that car?"

I had no idea.

"I was just a kid. My uncle ran the business until

I was old enough to take it over. And here I am. So, was he right? The truth is, I don't know. I don't really remember the things he used to say, and he's not here to say them now."

I wait, silent.

Alan comes back from his daydream. "Mark, I know you're young and optimistic, and I appreciate that. We like your energy here. But you have to understand that my father rode an economic and social wave. He surfed to success. He was always spouting off about his sales theories, but that's all they were. Theories."

I stay silent. What am I going to do? Tell him I spent yesterday afternoon with his dad? That I have clearer memories of Henry Langford than he does?

Alan sighs. "I don't want to bring you down, Mark. Just go easy on Earl, okay? He's all hat and no cattle, sometimes, but he's my biggest gun at the moment."

"Sure. And . . . I'm sorry. I guess I was just feeling a little punchy."

"Forget about it."

He pulls his chair closer into the desk and looks at his computer screen. The meeting is over. I turn to go.

"Mark?" I stop at the door. "You really want to help?" he asks. "Then help Trevor. That guy he spoke to for an hour the other day is actually coming back in today."

The surprise must be visible on my face.

"I know," he laughs. "Says he likes Trevor. Who knew? But if you want to help, then help him close that guy. It's just one car, but God knows the guy could use the confidence boost. I've got him doing more administrative work than sales, but I can't keep going with that forever. He has to learn to sell."

Or solve, I think to myself.

"Sure. I'll help him."

"Don't get cocky," he says. "Just support the guy. Frankly, Earl scares the crap out of him, and he could use someone he's comfortable with. He tells me you helped him before."

"I tried," I say, with a modest shrug, though I can feel the grin spreading across my face.

Alan glares at me. "I'm serious, Mark. You're on thin ice. Don't go jumping up and down."

My grin vanishes. I nod and step out of his office.

I walk back into the showroom. Earl is nowhere to be seen, but I'm keenly aware of the silence and the eyes on me.

I'm also aware that I almost just got my ass fired.

I need to get out of here. I know I need to sell, but right now I just need some air. I feel like I'm suffocating. I march past reception and straight out to the lot, then continue across the street toward downtown.

A few minutes later, I'm starting to calm down. I get a bite to eat, and to my surprise, I'm feeling pretty positive, and although I wouldn't say this to Alan, I'm excited about helping Trevor. My mental wheels are turning.

The customer likes Trevor. But as I've learned, someone liking you doesn't necessarily mean they'll buy from you. It helps, but it's not a dealmaker.

Trevor has got himself a real up, that's for sure. But as Henry said, an up is just an unidentified problem. If he's right, then as long as the problem stays unidentified, Trevor's not going to make the sale.

So how in the world does he find out what the problem is?

I don't know.

But I know someone who does.

***

The cellar is just as I left it. It's lost all of its original spookiness. And now that I've come to know the real thing, Cardboard Henry is nothing more than cardboard.

It takes me just a few moments to feed the broken film back into the projector and flip the switch . . .

"What the hell is that on your face?"

I shake off the disorientation and turn to find myself in the Langford showroom. The 1950s showroom, that is.

"What?"

"Kid, if I wanted you to look like a gorilla, I'd put you back in that suit."

"I—"

"You want to look like a hobo jumping a freight train," Henry says, "do it somewhere else. Otherwise, I'd suggest you get a shave."

Finally I catch on. The scrape on my face from the fall down the cellar stairs is freshly scabbed over and too sensitive to shave. I've got a good three days worth of stubble on there. Not a common look in 1957.

"Don't just stand there, kid. I'll give you a lift. I'm heading that way anyhow."

I follow Henry outside and around the side of the building. We pass the cellar doors, and I briefly wonder what's down there now, but then I stop short.

Henry is climbing into a Packard. *The* Packard. The one from the photo in Alan's office. The cream-colored top is down, and the entire enormous car gleams from head to tail.

"That's a beautiful car," I say.

"A 1950 Packard Custom Eight. They didn't even make one hundred of them," Henry says. "Too expensive. Nobody wanted them. I got this one at an auction for under two thousand."

If I could get this car back to the future, in this condition, it'd be worth two hundred thousand. Amazing.

"Jump in, kid. We aren't going far, but it's a great day for a drive."

I say a quick prayer that today isn't the day Henry dies at the wheel, then I hop in.

True to his word, we don't go far—just to the barbershop we passed on our trip to Ray's. We park in front, and Henry leaves the keys in the ignition. He holds open the door to the shop, and nods at me to enter.

We step into the comparatively cool and dark barbershop, and as my eyes adjust, we're greeted by an older gentleman in a white smock with a shock of matching white hair.

"Afternoon, Hank," says the man.

"Duncan. This is the new kid on the lot. Seems he forgot how to shave. Thought you might be able to help him out."

"Sure thing."

I sit in the chair, and Duncan pumps me up a few inches, reclines the seat, and drapes a fresh towel around my shoulders. A moment later, he cups a warm, damp cloth around my cheeks and chin. It feels fantastic.

"How's business?" Henry asks. He's taken a seat near the door and has a newspaper open.

"Good, good," Duncan says. "My boy says I should slow down. Enjoy my years, he says." Duncan breaks into a wheezy chuckle. "I told him I'd rust up solid if I ever stopped. I got the arthritis pretty bad, and it helps if I keep moving."

Duncan moves to the counter and begins to whisk up some shaving cream from a solid bar. I start to smile. I could get used to starting my day this way.

The grey-haired barber catches my eye in the mirror and smiles back. "You remind me of my boy," he says. "He was just here. He's a good boy. Gives me a lift to work when he can. He's trying to save my old knees from the walk, I suppose."

I can feel, more than hear, Henry's attention shift. Like the pressure in the room changed.

"Duncan," he says, "you're walking to work? From

your place?"

"The bus don't come by there no more. But I ain't no stranger to walking."

Duncan shuffles back toward me with a small brush and a dish full of foam.

Henry stays quiet as the old barber begins to lather my face and upper neck. At one point he nearly drops the bowl, and I see him wince with arthritic pain.

"Duncan," Henry says, "how long are you going to be able to keep showing up to work? How long can you walk three miles in the heat or the rain?"

Duncan's gnarled hand stops its brushing motion.

"To be honest, I don't know," he says at last. A shadow passes briefly over his face. "I can't imagine not coming here. All my friends are here."

I have a sudden image of an even older Duncan. Housebound. Lonely. Wasting away in some little house on the outskirts of the city.

"Those days your boy drives you," Hank says, "days like today, they better?"

"Surely. Days like this I cut hair all day. No nap." He looks at me in the mirror and winks.

"So if you can get a ride to work, you can earn more. Keep working longer—until you *want* to stop, not until you *have* to. Right?"

"I suppose," he says. "But he can't drive me all the time."

"Why don't you have your own car?"

Duncan laughs. "You're sounding like my boy now, Hank."

"What do you tell him when he asks?"

"The reason I don't have a car is the same reason you don't get a shave here twice a day, Hank. It ain't how I choose to spend my money."

"Maybe your boy's right, Duncan. That's a long walk. In this heat, it's not good for anyone."

"That may be, that may be," the barber says, then pauses. "I'll be honest with you, and I'll tell you what I can't tell my boy: it's money that I don't have."

"You can get a loan, Dunc. Finance the car."

He shakes his head. "I've never taken a loan in my life."

"What about this place? You own this building?"

"Got a mortgage," Duncan says. "But that's different. That's a business. Cars aren't a business." He laughs. "Well, I guess they are to you. But my business is hair."

"But if a car keeps you showing up here to cut hair, doesn't that make it business?"

Duncan doesn't reply. He shuffles over to the

counter and sets down the shaving cream. His hands shake gently. This guy must have been cutting hair since the fifties . . . No, wait. Since . . .

I realize with a jolt that Duncan could have been cutting hair at the turn of the century. My new barber might never have owned a car, but he might have been around when they were invented.

"Maybe so, Hank. Maybe so," Duncan says. "But I still don't have the money."

"You thought about using this place?" Henry asks. "The bank will lend you the money against it. The interest will be low—this is good collateral—and you'll get to keep working. You can probably make the payments just on the extra cuts and shaves you'll do by being here on time every day."

Duncan shakes his head gently, grins, and makes a clucking noise with his tongue. "Are you selling me, Henry Langford?"

"Nope. If I was, I'd tell you to let me finance it. I'd make more money, you'd pay more interest, and I'd sell you a car too."

I watch Duncan's face in the mirror. I can tell he's seriously considering Henry's words.

"What I'm telling you will keep you working longer," Henry continues. "It'll keep you safe and get you a car. You don't have to buy it from me."

With that, Henry stands up. "Got a quick errand to run, kid," he says. "I'll meet you out front. Make him respectable if you can, Dunc."

Henry steps outside, and the bells above the door jingle.

"Aren't you going to ask me?" Duncan says to my reflection.

"Ask you what?"

"If I'm buying a car from Hank," he says.

I think about that. "I guess I am curious," I say. "But I have two questions, not one."

"Shoot," the old mans says.

"If you were going to buy a car, would you buy it from Henry?"

He replies immediately. "Of course." He says it like it's a statement of the obvious. Like of course fish need water.

"Okay. Second question, then. Why him?"

"Why Hank?" The barber wheezes out a laugh. "Easy. He knows when to open his ears and quiet his mouth. He might talk a lot sometimes, but he knows when to clam up too."

Duncan begins to strop a straight razor. The tremble in his hands suddenly seems to me to be a little more pronounced, and I force myself to look away.

"And...and that makes you trust him? Clamming up?"

He chuckles. "Hell no! Plenty of crooked silent types in the world." Duncan approaches me with the straight razor. His hand is shaking noticeably.

I'm suddenly feeling very nervous. "You know...I have this...I hurt my chin. The other day."

Duncan chuckles. "You might say selling a car is a little bit like getting a shave." He closes in on my neck with the razor, which is jumping around like a fish on a line.

"Sometimes you gotta talk," he says. "Other times you gotta hush up. The good ones know the difference."

I clamp my jaw shut as the shaking blade approaches my neck.

Then, at the last second, the tremor vanishes from his hands. With practiced strokes, the old man quickly dispatches the stubble from my face. The scab on my chin stays untouched.

Duncan wipes the remaining smudges of shaving cream from my cheeks and neck. He removes the towel from my shoulders with a flourish, and I stand up.

Duncan moves to the cash register, and it's only then that I realize I don't have any 1950s cash on me. I pat my pockets, wondering how to navigate the problem.

"Tell Hank to pay me next time he's in," Duncan says, rescuing me. "And tell him okay."

"Okay?"

"I'm going to the bank right now. Tell him I'll be in at the end of the day to pick something out."

***

Henry seems pleased but unsurprised by the news. I'm amazed. He just sold a car sight unseen in a barbershop. I get the impression, though, that this is not an uncommon occurrence.

"I feel like a drive," Henry says, as we walk down the sidewalk toward the Packard. "Why don't you ride along?"

A few moments later he points the big car away from the dealership, and we head due south.

The town quickly fades away, and in what seems like minutes, we're passing farm after farm. The roads are nearly deserted. I know this will all be suburbia in my time. It's hard to believe so much will change.

I settle back into my seat and enjoy the breeze in my hair. I recount to Henry what Duncan said about sales.

"You think it's that simple?" I ask. "What Duncan said? Knowing when to shut up?"

"No," Henry says. "I think it's like most things. When you get good at them, they look simple."

I think of Trevor. And myself. "But what if you're not good at them?"

"That's what we're working on, kid."

In a hell of a roundabout way, I add silently, looking at the scenery around me. I decide to cut to the chase.

"So how do I get customers to tell me their problems?"

"You can't get them to."

"Then how do I find out?"

"They'll tell you."

"But you just said I can't get them to tell me."

"You can't."

This is crazy.

Henry laughs and turns up the radio. "Don't you just love selling cars?" he shouts, then puts the pedal down.

We fly down the road, the wind in our hair. When the song ends, Henry turns down the radio and settles back in his seat.

"Here's the thing," he says. "You can't get customers to tell you their problem. You can't make them."

"But I can get them to want to?"

"That's part of it, for sure. But you've got a bigger problem to solve first."

"What's that?"

"You can't solve a problem you don't care about."

"But I do care. That's the whole point. I'm not one of those sleazy sales guys who doesn't care."

"I believe you, kid. The trouble is that customers won't. They're used to being sold. Being gamed. Being pitched."

Henry glances in his rear-view mirror.

"You remember first gear?" he asks.

"Sure. Stop selling and start solving."

"Right. That was about shifting how you see the goal of sales. What about second gear?"

"Umm . . . shift from confrontation to collaboration. That's about changing how you see the customer."

"Right. Good work. Seeing them differently is a hell of a start. Now you need to start treating them differently too. You need to prove you care. Only after you prove that you're different, that you care about them and their situation, will they start to see you differently."

"How do I do that?"

"There's only one way to show people that you really care, kid—and it's not to kiss their behinds. It's not to give them prizes or cut your prices, either. It's to be interested in them—to ask questions and be genuinely interested in the answers.

"Like you did with Duncan."

Henry nods. "That's the shift into third gear. You shift from pitching to probing."

The fields are gradually starting to give way to houses and industrial areas. Commercial buildings, like feedlots and granaries, sprout from the flat earth.

"Pitching is sales," Henry continues. "Probing is about searching for problems to solve. And the heart of probing—the heart of caring—is asking questions."

"Asking questions," I repeat to myself. As usual, Henry seems to have a knack for boiling things down to their essence.

"You have to get curious to be in this business. You have to really care about the problem you need to solve. Anybody can pretend they care, but the people who really do? You'll know them because they ask questions."

I ponder this for a moment.

"Can it really be that simple?"

Henry laughs. "Yes, it can be that simple, kid. But that doesn't mean it's easy. You'd be surprised how hard it is to ask an honest question—how difficult it is for people to be truly interested in someone else."

It's not hard to see the truth in that. People can be pretty self-absorbed, I think.

"It takes practice to ask instead of tell. Questions show you care. They prove that you're interested. But there's more to it than that. You need to ask strategic questions."

"Strategic?"

"Sure. We're trying to find a problem, not ask about the weather. This isn't about small talk. It's about solving a mystery."

Solving a mystery, I think. I like that. And it sure seems a lot more interesting than what Earl's been trying to teach me.

I turn in my seat to face Henry. "So how do I ask strategic questions?"

"Easy. Before anything comes out of your mouth, rephrase it as a question. It's that simple. You don't tell someone they need a car. You ask them how a car would make their life better."

I think back to how Henry asked Duncan whether

a car would help him keep doing what he loves. And how he asked him if he could see financing a car as a business decision, not a personal one. In hindsight, the questions helped Duncan sell the idea to himself.

"So I should just rephrase everything as a question?"

Henry nods. "Resist the urge to tell and sell. Ears open; mouth closed, kid. That's how sales work. Ask your question, then shut up and get out of the way."

"Then I have one more question."

"Shoot."

"Can I call you Hank?"

"No."

And with that, the radio goes up, the pedal goes down, and we head for town.

The timing couldn't be better. I need to get back to the Langford of my time.

THIRD GEAR

The Shift: From Pitching to Probing

*Asking questions shows genuine interest
and helps reveal the customer's true problem.*

CHAPTER 7

FOURTH GEAR

I don't skip a beat when I arrive back in the cellar. Now, back in my own time, I check my watch. Trevor's guy could be here any minute, so I bound up the stairs, jog around the corner, and head inside.

"Hey, Mark," Jennifer greets me. "You missed an up. Rusty took her."

I look out the window. Rusty is standing next to a woman in a business suit. He's got the hood open on a luxury sedan, and I can see him pointing at the engine. She couldn't care less. She's looking at her phone.

There's an up I'll never get back. She'll be gone in minutes. But maybe I can still help Trevor.

I find him in the shop.

"Hey, Mark," he says with a grin. "Guess who's coming back today?"

"I heard. That's great news. What are you going to do with him this time?"

"I figured I'd just use your system. You know—don't sell him. Just talk."

Jennifer's voice comes over the loudspeaker. "Trevor to the showroom."

Trevor smiles, "That must be him. Gotta go."

"Wait." I grab his arm. "How about this time you . . . you talk to him a little differently?"

"Differently? Why? It worked great last time."

"Just trust me."

"I gotta go, Mark. He's waiting."

"Look, Trevor. Do one thing for me. Just . . . ask questions."

"Ask questions?"

How do I get this across to him in ten seconds? Then I hear the echo of Henry's voice in my mind.

This isn't about small talk. It's about solving a mystery.

"Pretend . . . pretend it's a mystery. Like in those

detective novels you're always reading. Only instead of a murder, the mystery is that . . . is that there's something stopping him from buying a car, and you need to find out what it is by asking him questions."

Trevor looks at me like I've lost my mind. "Why is it a mystery? The guy needs a car. What's the big deal? Maybe if he likes me enough, he'll buy it here. End of story. I gotta go."

And with that, Trevor jogs off toward the showroom. And so begins another lost sale.

***

I can't stand the thought of watching Trevor blow another sale. And my stomach is grumbling. Time travel is hungry business.

As I walk to the deli, I'm struck again by how different things are from 1957. Even the air is different. Stale, somehow. The sidewalks are busy, but now no one looks at each other. There's more traffic too, but for some reason it seems quieter.

I can't put my finger on it at first, but then it hits me. There's no music.

Every car has air conditioning now. All the windows are rolled up. In Henry's time, I heard dozens of cars blaring the same music at the same time, courtesy of AM radio.

By the time I eat lunch and wander back to the dealership, I've been gone for over an hour. Suddenly, I feel a pang of anxiety. I haven't really worked all week. I've taken no ups, and it feels like I've spent more time in 1957 than I have here.

The anxious feeling vanishes as I step through the front doors of the dealership. As it turns out, no one else is working either.

There's a small party going on. Everyone's milling about the reception desk smiling. All the salespeople are there, and Alan's emerged from his office. I look at Jennifer.

"Trevor made a sale," she says. She remains unimpressed, as usual, but the rest of the team is jubilant.

My first thought is that it's a lot of celebration for one car. But then I realize that everyone wants to support Trevor. He's a good guy. Even Earl seems genuinely happy. Whether it's for Trevor or just because the week's no-sale streak is broken, I don't know, but at least he's smiling instead of glowering at me.

That smile vanishes as soon as Trevor opens his mouth.

"It's really Mark who deserves the credit," he says. "He told me exactly what to do."

I try to deflect the praise—I'm not sure I even believe it, let alone deserve it—but I can see Earl start to smoulder. And I can see Alan tuning in from the corner of my eye.

We mill about for a while longer, but Trevor's comment seems to have changed the mood somehow. A few minutes later, everyone begins to drift back to their desks.

Trevor pulls me aside.

"I really meant that, Mark," he says. "I did what you told me. The bit about the mystery." He looks at the floor. "I felt a bit silly, but I pretended I was a detective, like you said. I asked him questions."

"And it worked?"

He nods, looking incredulous.

I'm a bit shocked myself. Despite everything, I think I'm having more trouble believing in Henry's system than I am in believing that I've actually been talking to him.

"It turns out the guy had some credit problems," Trevor says, the pride evident in his voice. "He was embarrassed. That's why he came back—because he felt comfortable with me. But if I hadn't asked the questions, he might never have told me. Turns out the credit problem was smaller than he thought. And now his problem is solved, thanks to you."

"I really can't take credit for that," I say.

Really.

I can't.

***

Earl's on point. The floor is quiet, but a few minutes later, I see him perk up when a father-son team arrives on the lot. He smooths his hair and is out the door in a flash.

The minute he's gone, Rusty's at my desk.

"Trevor told me what you said. How you helped him."

"I don't know if it was really me."

Rusty ignores me and presses on. "That woman I was talking to this morning. She kept talking about the price, and I tried to show her the specs—that the car is really worth the money—but she just kept saying it was too much."

"Uh, that's too bad."

"Yeah, well . . . I wanted to ask you . . . what should

I have done?"

Huh? I have yet to sell a single car, and now people are coming to me for sales advice?

"I'm not sure how to help," I say. "I told Trevor all I know."

"I know what you told Trevor. It makes sense. But I already know the problem. The problem is the price. I tried to get Alan to move on it, but he wouldn't."

I can see where this is going. And I don't like it.

"So . . . can you just talk to him? To Alan? We all know he likes you. Can you ask him to be more flexible? We need more room on the sticker price, or we're just not going to be able to sell cars."

This is not a good idea. I know that. But guys who wear gorilla suits aren't good at saying no.

So I don't.

***

This time, when I knock on the door, Alan looks up with a smile.

"Good job, Mark. Thanks for helping Trevor." After a pause, he adds, "And me."

I look at the picture on the wall. Henry with the Packard.

"I really can't take the credit," I say.

"Suit yourself. What can I do for you?"

I step all the way in and close the door.

"I need to talk to you about something."

"Shoot."

"I . . . I was wondering about the pricing. It's been a bit slow. I was thinking . . . maybe we could be more flexible. Maybe move a bit more inventory as a result."

Alan sighs and swivels around to face me directly.

"The short answer? No way. Lowering prices is a race to the bottom. And the reality is there's just not that much margin. I haven't got much room to move."

I suspected as much. At least I tried.

I'm about to leave, when I take one more glance at the framed photo on the wall.

"Hey . . . Alan?"

"Hmm?" He's gone back to his paperwork.

"What do you think your dad would have thought of all this? I mean, about the car business these days?"

Alan sighs. "Who knows? He died when I was a kid."

I nod and turn to leave, but Alan stops me.

"Mark, I wish my dad was here to guide this place, but he isn't. I wish he'd been here to guide me as a young man, but he wasn't. I wish I could set the price of a car any way I like, but I can't. There are some things you just can't do." He pauses and smiles. "But you can tell Rusty you tried."

I look up at him in surprise. "How'd you know?"

"I might not have Henry Langford here, Mark. But I wasn't born yesterday." He swivels his chair back to his computer screen. "Tell Rusty we're not slashing prices."

I leave the office knowing I've fulfilled my obligation to Rusty but feeling vaguely dissatisfied too. I understand what Alan's saying. I know the basic economics of the business, and there really isn't that much room to move on price. Still, what Rusty is saying makes some sense too. Every single customer that comes in here seems to be looking for a deal. They all want the lowest price in town.

I can't help wondering what Henry would say about that.

But... I don't have to wonder, do I?

***

A few minutes later, I'm slipping out of the showroom with 1957 on my mind. Now that Rusty's planted the pricing issue in my head, I'm dying to know what Henry has to say about it.

I don't get more than a few steps from the front door when I'm stopped by a voice.

"Excuse me? Buddy?"

A stout man in a jacket and jeans is standing near the first row of cars. He must have just arrived on the lot because he's not even on Jennifer's radar yet.

He waves me over.

"What can I do for you?" I ask.

"Yeah. How much is this one?"

I look in the direction of his outstretched arm. It's a new arrival on the lot—a minivan. There's no sticker on the windshield, but I know the price and I tell him.

"Huh." He seems surprised, but I'm not sure if it's the cheaper-than-I-thought kind of surprise or the you-gotta-be-kidding-me type.

I don't have to wait long to find out.

"They've got the same thing at that place up on High Street. It's less."

Before I can get too caught up in pricing, I introduce myself.

"And you need a van, specifically?" I ask.

"Yep."

"We just got this in. To be honest, I haven't even

been in it yet. Why don't I grab the keys and we can take it out?"

"Why?"

His question catches me off guard.

"Well . . . to see if you like it."

"I already like it. I told you I looked at it across town."

"Right. You did tell me that."

"Can you match the price?"

My first instinct is to say yes. I desperately need a sale. Then I think back to what Alan just told me ten minutes ago.

Tell Rusty we're not slashing prices.

"I can't promise to match it," I say. "But if you want to come inside, we can look at the numbers."

The man sticks out his hand and my stomach falls. I shake it reluctantly.

"That's okay," he says. "If you can't, you can't. Thanks for your time, Mark."

And before I can say another word, he's on his way back across the lot to where his car is parked.

The price issue just landed a lot closer to home.

***

I slink quietly back into the showroom.

Rusty and Trevor look up at me expectantly, but go back to their work when they see my face.

Another up, gone. Another sale, blown. Another day, over.

I slump into my chair. The excitement I felt just a few minutes ago—about Henry's ideas, about the potential to do better and make Charlotte proud of me—it's all drained away, siphoned off by yet another failure.

Even Trevor is selling more than me.

I hang my head in my hands. I realize, to my chagrin, that I am actually close to tears.

I imagine what I must look like to the others. I'm a joke, the kind that doesn't make you laugh but just makes you squirm nervously in your seat.

I need to go home.

The instant the thought of home enters my mind, the memory of this morning surfaces, pushing aside everything else.

I'm going to be a father.

How could I have forgotten? With everything that's happened, it just slipped my mind. I suppose a guy who discovers time travel might be forgiven the odd mental lapse, but still . . .

What kind of a father will I be when I start by forgetting my own child within the first hour of parenthood?

***

Charlotte is feeling better when I get home but is clearly not herself. She's made dinner, which is a good sign, but isn't speaking to me in sentences longer than three words, which is a bad one.

"Good day?" she asks.

"Busy."

"You shaved."

I nod and feel my smooth cheeks. I'm about to tell her I got a real shave downtown, but then I realize I could never explain it.

"Any sales?" she asks.

My stomach drops. I'm not sure how to reply to this. I mean, I know the answer, but 'no' doesn't capture the entire story.

I did do some sales training in 1957 with a dead guy . . . Does that count as sales?

I opt for changing the subject.

"How are you feeling?"

"Not nauseous."

I take a deep breath. I need to turn this around. I think back to the Third Shift and what I learned this morning.

"So . . . I guess we should start a college fund," I say brightly. "What do you think?"

"With what?" Charlotte asks. "Food stamps?"

I don't care what Henry Langford says. Questions don't always get you the answers you want to hear.

***

The next morning, it's Charlotte who sleeps in, and I decide the best thing I can do at this point is get to work. I leave a note saying I have an early sales appointment.

The way I look at it, it's not exactly lying.

Right?

I arrive in 1957 bracing myself for either the sound of Henry's whistle shrieking in my ear or some kind of command beginning with the word "kid." Instead, I find myself alone in the showroom.

Or, at least I think I'm alone.

I hear a skittering sound, and a tiny toy car slides across the showroom floor and stops against the side of my shoe.

I look around, but the room is empty.

"Hello?"

Silence.

I turn in the direction the toy came from. Then I slowly drop to my hands and knees and peer under the nearest car.

A small face peers back.

"Hey," I say.

The face belongs to a young boy. He's freckled. Serious. He holds a finger to his lips. "Shhhhh."

I mouth the word "o-kay" and stand up.

A moment later, there's a creak, and the boy emerges from behind the car, pulling a red wagon full of toy cars.

"Hi," I whisper.

The boy looks me over. Then his eyes move past me, darting about the room. He tightens his grip on the wagon handle.

"I'm Mark. You don't need to be scared."

Just then the door chime tinkles, and the boy's eyes widen. In a panic, he turns and bolts, wagon in tow, across the showroom floor, making a beeline for the room where the projector is set up. He reaches the door in a flash but misjudges the angle of the wagon.

There's a crash as the wagon smashes into the door-frame, spilling toy cars across the floor.

The boy turns, a look of horror on his face. He begins to frantically scoop the fallen cars back into the wagon.

"Hey!" a voice booms out.

I turn to see Henry striding across the showroom floor. "How many times have I told you that you can't play in here?" Henry looks down at the spilled cars, then at the doorframe. There's a huge gouge in the wood where the metal wagon hit.

Henry shakes his head in frustration.

"Come with me," he says.

Henry marches toward the front door of the dealership. The boy gives me a sad glance, and then hangs his head and shuffles after him.

I bend to pick up the rest of the toy cars, then tuck the wagon into the projection room and close the door. I can see Henry outside lecturing the boy.

And then it hits me. It's Alan.

I wait a few minutes. Then I head outside. Henry is leaning against the Packard, smoking. Alan is nowhere to be seen.

"He ran that wagon into the side of a brand new

Buick last summer," he says. "Cost me a fortune. Kid never learns."

I don't know what to say.

"Boys will be boys," I manage at last.

"So they say," he says. "But I think I'll do a lot better with him when he's your age. Maybe we'll see eye to eye then."

It's all I can do not to spill everything. Henry, you're not going to see him when he's my age. Don't be too harsh.

Henry saves me. "What's on your mind, kid? We going to solve a few problems today?"

I shake off the image of young Alan.

"Can I ask you something?"

"You practicing asking questions?"

I grin. "Well, I guess I am trying to solve a bit of a mystery." I think back to my up from the previous day—the one who wanted to buy the minivan. "What do you think about lowering prices? It seems like everyone just wants a lower price."

Henry seems to think deeply, taking several long drags on his cigarette. It's the longest I've ever seen him take to answer a question.

"This car," he says at last, patting the hood, "well, not this one, but Packard in general, used to be the luxury car maker. I guess Cadillac has that crown now, but for a time, it was Packard."

"Okay."

"So what do you think happened to them?"

I know exactly what happened—or at least I know enough to know that Packard isn't making cars in my time—but I decide it's best to keep that to myself.

"Well," Henry says, "for starters, they made this damn thing."

"What's the matter with it?"

"Nothing's the matter with it, kid. Fine car. Did you know this car was the most expensive production car built in America in 1950? The most expensive. But I bet they never made more than eighty or a hundred of them. Know why?"

"Because the price was too high."

"No, it's because the value was too low. In the case of this Packard, people could buy the next model down and get pretty much all the same features. So why buy the Custom Eight? It wasn't worth it. The value wasn't there."

I think this through for a moment. "So why not just drop the price? Then the value goes up, right?"

"I see you took some math in college too," Henry ribs. "Yes, kid. Of course. Drop the price and the value goes up. But value isn't just about lowering prices. Look at Duncan the barber. Why would anyone pay for a shave? Hell, you can shave your own face for free. Cheapest price there is. Can't beat that for value."

I think back to how great it felt to have a professional shave. "I guess people are still paying because he gives them something they can't give themselves for free," I acknowledge.

Henry nods. "What about Ray? People could make their own floats at home if they wanted to save money."

"But you wouldn't get the same experience staying home." I say.

Henry slaps me on the back. "That's just it, kid. Some things matter more than price. Low price only matters when there's no other value."

"Other value?"

"Ray gives value by listening and solving problems. You know, giving advice. You saw the kids in there."

He's right. There was practically a line-up of teenagers wanting to talk to him.

"Same with Duncan," Henry continues. "You think people can't shave themselves? Of course they can. But Duncan can shave you closer than you can on your own and make you feel important at the same time. That's worth two bits any day."

"Those are all types of value?"

"Value comes in a lot of packages. Trust. Advice. A solution to a problem. Convenience. There are a million ways to create value, kid. What you need to remember is this—people pay for value. In fact, they pay more for it."

I find myself nodding. Once again, Henry's point is hard to dispute.

"People will only pay so much for a car—look at this Packard. It's a perfect example. But they'll pay more for a solution. They'll pay more to work with someone who will help them get what they really want or to avoid something they don't want."

"And people don't want to be sold," I say, thinking back to the first shift

He points his whistle at me. "You better believe it. People will pay more to avoid being sold. That's why we don't trade on price, kid. We trade on value."

It's starting to make sense. Maybe there really is a way to avoid cutting prices.

He pats the hood of the Packard. "Me, I'll pay for beauty. So until this lady finds her way to the junk-yard, I'll get value from her every time I look out the window."

"So beauty, trust, advice, experience . . . there's a lot of ways to create value then."

"An endless number, kid. Like grains of sand on the beach. But they all share one thing in common. They're about deciding what you can give, not what you can get. Most salesmen are focused on getting the sale. The best ones, though, they're focused on giving value."

He looks past me, and I turn to see a customer wandering the lot inspecting vehicles.

"Come on, kid. Let's go give some value."

He steps on his cigarette butt and walks away.

I follow behind, but not before catching a glimpse of Alan around the corner of the building, his face streaked with tears.

***

My arrival back in the Langford cellar is more unsettling than what I've become used to.

Physically, it's no different. A strange sort of fading out of the hard things in one place—floors and furniture and things I might be touching—replaced by the sensations of the new things of where (when?) I've arrived.

What *is* different, though, is that I'm feeling guilty. Seeing Alan and watching how he interacted with his father feels like an intrusion. Like spying.

As I walk up the cellar steps, I push the thought from my mind and think about Rusty. I have to let him know that Alan won't move on the price issue. But if what Henry said is true—that people will pay for value—then perhaps somewhere in that truth is the answer to Rusty's dilemma.

I emerge into bright sunlight and squint as my eyes adjust. I'm stooping to grab the cellar door when a voice startles me.

"So that's where you've been hiding," comes a gruff drawl.

I turn to see Earl leaning against the corner of the building smoking a cigarette. My heart is hammering in my chest.

"Oh ... hey, Earl. How's it going?"

He flashes me a friendly grin. "You tell me, college boy. You seem to have me all figured out."

"Look, I'm sorry about that. I was kind of upset about the whole gorilla suit thing. I shouldn't have taken it out on you like that."

"Why not?" The grin vanishes, like it just fell through a trapdoor in his face. "Seems like you know better—like you're some super salesman now. Got people coming to you. Got the boss's ear."

I don't like where this is heading.

"I was just trying to help," I say.

Earl flicks his cigarette and steps away from the building. Toward me.

"Where'd you learn this help?" he asks. "Your rich daddy-in-law?" His eyes narrow. "No, I don't think so. If he was that helpful, you'd be working at one of his dealerships, wouldn't you?"

I say nothing.

"I thought so. This is just a case of too-big-for-your-britches, ain't that right?"

I keep my mouth shut, anxious for the confrontation to be over.

Earl looks down at the open cellar door.

"What's down there?"

My mind races.

"Uh, nothing . . . just boxes of junk," I say. "I thought maybe I could find some old pictures of the dealership or something—maybe give one to Alan as a gift, you know?"

He scrutinizes me. Then his smile returns. "A gift, huh? A little more sunshine to blow up the boss's ass, right?" He chuckles. "Well, I'll tell you what. Why

"Right," says Trevor. "We could give them an upgrade on the sound system or a better option package up for the same price."

"That stuff costs money too," says Jennifer, who's drifted over from reception. "You won't be able to convince Alan to pay for that any more than you can convince him to drop the price."

I smile at her. "That's right. Those are all good ideas to make the car more valuable. But what if the value doesn't have to be in the car?"

Trevor stares at me blankly.

Rusty looks at me like I've just burned the flag.

"But that's what we do, man," Rusty says. "We sell cars."

"Or at least we try to," Trevor adds helpfully.

"Yes," I agree. "But what if the value isn't just in the car? What if it's somewhere else too?"

The two of them stare back at me. Trevor blinks.

Jennifer snorts. "You two are idiots."

I look over at her, half-shocked and half-amused. I step back just a bit. This could be good.

"What?" she demands. "You've all got your heads up your tailpipes. You think everything is about the damn car. I can tell you right now it isn't."

Now we're all staring at her.

"It's true," she continues. "And I'll prove it to you." She looks around the showroom, then lowers her voice. "You want to know where I bought my last car?"

"From your brother," Rusty says. "You told us he basically gave it to you."

"Well, I lied. I bought it at Donovan's."

Silence.

Donovan's is a dealership across town. A competitor. A much-despised competitor, in fact.

Rusty's mouth is opening and closing like he wants to speak but can't.

"I know, I know," she says. "But you guys just kept ... not helping me. It was my first car ever. I didn't know what to do or what I wanted, and you guys were just telling me what to get. You never even asked me any questions—you just droned on endlessly about stupid technical stuff and how great a deal you could get me."

"Jennifer," Rusty says evenly, "how much did you pay for that car?"

She tells him the price. His jaw drops. "Are you kid—"

"Just never mind, Rusty," she says. "I know I paid more, and I don't care. In fact, I'm happy I did."

Trevor looks like he's struggling for air.

She turns to me. "I know what you're talking

about," she says. "About value. I went to Donovan's because they made it easy. They helped me decide. They made me feel smart, even though I didn't know anything. They helped me get the exact right car for me. And I love it. I paid more, and I'll tell you what, I'd do it all over again."

We're all speechless.

"And another thing," she says. "You know what the hardest part of buying my car at Donovan's was? Having to think up some lame excuse just to make you dorks feel better."

Then she turns on her heels and marches away.

"Can you believe that?" Rusty says.

"You better," I tell him. "That's the kind of value I'm talking about."

Rusty shakes his head. "Are you telling me that every customer is as crazy as her? That they don't care about price?"

"Of course they care about price," I say. "And of course there has to be value in the cars. But we need to add value to the experience of buying them too. We have to solve problems. Make it easy to buy. We have to make people feel they can trust us."

Rusty is still looking at me like I'm speaking a foreign language, and I try to simplify as much as possible.

"We have to really understand what people need, then give them good advice about how to get it," I tell him. "We don't have to make buying a car from us cheaper. We have to make buying a car from us better."

Trevor has been leaning back in his chair, just watching. He finally speaks up. "So . . . part of what they're buying is . . . is the experience of buying?"

I smile. "That's a good way to put it. And unless you want to argue about price and cut commissions for the rest of your life, then yes—the experience of buying a car here needs to be worth something."

Now that I've articulated it, I can see it clearly. I grab a pen and a pad of paper.

"If we want people to spend top dollar here, then we need to focus on value. In our case, that looks like this."

I turn the pad sideways and scribble on it:

VALUE = PRODUCT + BUYING EXPERIENCE

I circle PRODUCT. "This is the car: the price, the features, the ride, the new car smell. But we can only do so much with that. We've only got so much inventory, and we can only move so much on price."

Trevor is nodding.

"And that means," I tap BUYING EXPERIENCE with my pen, "we need to work on this. That's where we create the extra value."

Rusty tilts his head to one side as he looks at the pad of paper. I can see I'm finally getting through to his mechanical mind.

It occurs to me that I should call Jennifer back over to tell us more about her buying experience, but before I have the chance, the door from the lot opens and Earl walks in.

I'm immediately self-conscious. I lower the pad to my side, but Earl just walks briskly past us without so much as a glance.

We watch as he strides into Alan's office and shuts the door behind him.

FOURTH GEAR

The Shift: From Getting to Giving

*Giving real value allows you to
earn respect and sales.*

CHAPTER 8
FIFTH GEAR

I'm awakened the next morning by the ring of my cell phone. I jerk upright in a panic—sure that I'm late for work again, but it's barely light out.

I fumble for my phone. It's the dealership.

What the hell?

"Mark? It's Alan. Can you come in a bit early? I'd like to speak with you."

I flash back to the previous afternoon when Earl blew us off and disappeared into Alan's office. This can't be good.

"Sure," I say.

I shower in record time. Charlotte's still not really

talking to me, so there's little morning conversation to slow me down. I briefly debate trying out Henry's fourth shift with her, but I don't even know where to begin. Instead, I grab a quick cup of coffee and race off to work.

Despite the early hour, the humidity hangs in the air like a blanket. It's the first of September and just a few days since my collapse in the parking lot, but it feels like this heat wave has lasted for months.

My mind is racing as I make the familiar drive to the dealership. Alan's never called me in early. Am I being fired? Am I in trouble? Earl must have screwed me over somehow. Well, maybe Earl's right—maybe I am too big for my britches. Maybe Alan's going to knock me down a peg.

The drive seems to take forever. I keep telling myself that I've done nothing wrong, but this feels like bad news.

***

Alan looks up as I knock on the open door.

"Thanks for coming in, Mark. I appreciate it. Sit down."

I pull up a chair.

"I spoke with Earl yesterday."

Uh oh.

"Seems someone stopped into the lot yesterday. New guy in town."

"Yeah. I saw him. Did Earl sell him a car?"

"No. That's why you're here."

"Alan, I can't take Earl's lead."

"It's not exactly Earl's anymore."

"He messed it up?"

"Far from it. In fact, he landed it right on my desk."

"I'm not sure I'm following you. I thought he didn't sell the guy a car," I say.

"He didn't. It's a fleet account. A new company coming to the city. They got a tax incentive to set up a new headquarters here."

"So . . . they need a company car?"

"No," he says. "They don't need *a* car. They need *twenty-seven* of them."

My mouth falls open. "Wow."

Alan nods. "Yeah. It's an important account. All the service that comes with it, plus all the promotional value. It's not going to make or break us, but it'll definitely make a difference here."

"So . . . how can I help?"

"For this kind of deal, everyone's going to pull out their best prices—us included. But that's not enough. I overheard you talking with Trevor and Rusty yesterday, and I think maybe you can help."

"How?"

"Close this deal. Make it happen." He sees my expression and raises a hand, "Don't worry—Earl will still get his commission and be around to help. But I want this to go through, and we both know that Earl isn't the guy to make it happen."

This is nuts.

"I . . . I don't know. Why me? What do I know about closing?"

Alan smiles. "I asked myself the same question this morning."

He pauses, as if he's not exactly sure how to explain it. He gets up and paces the room, finally stopping in front of the picture of Henry with the Packard.

"He's been on my mind a lot lately," he says at last. "My father. Today's the anniversary of his death, so that could have something to do with it, but . . . I don't know."

He turns back to me.

"You know why I feel I should ask you to help? The

answer is that I think my father would have."

I'm speechless.

"The last few days, it just feels like part of him is here. Maybe it's all the questions you've been asking. The things you've been saying to the team. I didn't know my father for long, but it's like his voice is echoing through this place again."

You don't know the half of it.

He looks me in the eye. "The short answer is I don't know what you know about closing, but it just feels right to ask you to be a part of this. Just contribute if you can. The guy is coming back in later today, and I'd like you to be here to meet with him."

Alan sits and turns back to his computer. It's clear he's said all he wants to, so I turn to go.

On my way out, I notice for the first time that there's a large gouge in the wooden trim around his office door. It's been painted over who knows how many times, but it's still recognizable.

It's where Alan's wagon crashed into it in 1957.

***

I spend most of the morning in a daze.

This is crazy. I don't know a thing about closing—I'm the new guy. In comparison to the others, my sales don't even register on the graph. Not only that, but I'm the youngest on the team. Shouldn't someone besides 'College Boy' be doing this?

Then I remember Earl, and my stomach drops a little further still. He's going to lose his mind. If he doesn't completely loathe me already, he will soon.

And what happens if I screw it up? I'll be sending thousands and thousands of dollars down the drain. I'd be signing my own walking papers.

No. I'm not a closer. I just follow. I'm the guy who wears the gorilla suit. I just say yes.

But even as I think this, there's a part of me that knows it's not true. It's a small part, yes, but it's growing. It's the part that knows with certainty that Henry is right. It's the same part of me that knows that falling into that cellar was about falling down the rabbit hole and leaving part of the old me behind forever.

But whether I'm a closer or not, my mind is already working on how to get this deal done. I review Henry's shifts in my mind.

First gear: shift from selling to solving.
Second gear: shift from confrontation to collaboration.
Third gear: shift from pitching to probing.
Fourth gear: shift from getting to giving.

I roll the ideas around in my head. They all make sense. They all fit. What's more, I've seen them all work to create stronger relationships with customers and to bring out an honorable side of sales that I wasn't sure even existed.

But none of that is helping me right now. In a few hours, there'll be a customer here that needs not just one car, but cars. He's got the money. He wants to buy. He will buy.

But we're competing with dealerships across the city.

So how do I close them?

That has to be the final shift.

Closing must be fifth gear. It's time to find Henry Langford again.

Even as the thought registers in my mind, I realize that my feet are already in motion. I'm outside the building and heading toward the storm cellar.

I'm about to turn the corner, but something is nagging at me. The chip in Alan's door. I saw it happen in 1957. And here it is today.

That makes sense. It should still be there.

Shouldn't it?

But would the chip have happened at all if I hadn't been there that day? If I hadn't been talking to young Alan, would he have been caught by his father? Would he have crashed the wagon into the doorframe?

Did I change what happened that day?

I stop dead in my tracks.

By traveling back to 1957, have I changed today? I try to remember if I ever saw that mark on the doorframe before this week, but I just don't know.

The whole idea starts to make my brain hurt, and I force my feet back into forward motion. What else have I changed without realizing it? What if getting a shave in 1957 delayed someone else's shave, and then they were hit by a car crossing the street? Or something worse? What if a little thing I do in 1957 changes all of history?

My head is spinning, but it clears the instant I round the corner of the building.

Something is wrong.

The cellar doors are open.

I closed them. I know I did. Earl was here, and I closed the door so that he wouldn't . . .

Oh, God.

***

It's a beautiful summer day in 1957, and the Langford lot is packed. I've never seen anything like it.

What the hell is going on?

There's a carnival atmosphere—music is playing, kids are engaged in midway games, families are strolling the lot. I can smell hamburgers.

There are picnic tables scattered near the service station, and I see Ray has set up a temporary soda stand against the building. I wave to him, and he flashes me a smile before turning his attention back to the line of thirsty customers in front of him.

I look up. A banner announcing Langford's customer appreciation day hangs overhead. It's the annual company picnic, charity fundraiser, and all-around good time. I've seen lots of photos of it. It happened every year on the same day—the first day of September.

But this picnic is different. It's Henry's last. If the story, as I know it, is true, then Henry Langford will die in the twisted wreckage of a beautiful 1950 Packard Custom Eight in just a few hours.

The thought sends a pang of sadness through my gut, but it vanishes as I'm startled by a firm slap on my back.

"There you are, kid," booms a familiar voice.

Henry's clearly had a beer or two. Or more. He's brimming with good cheer. I've never seen him so happy. That's great for him. But not so great for me because I've got a couple of problems.

The first is that I need some time alone with Henry, and he's going to be a man in demand today. In fact, he's already got his hand clamped on the shoulder of the man next to him.

The second problem is that the man next to him is Earl Cochrane.

**

The only thing more shocking than seeing Earl here is seeing how damn composed he is. Having suddenly traveled back in time to 1957 doesn't seem to have fazed him at all. He actually seems excited to be here.

"Well, here he is now," Earl says, beaming at me.

"Kid," says Hank, "I was just talking to your cousin, here. Apparently he's in sales too. You never told me it runs in the family."

Earl winks at me.

"Right. I guess I forgot to mention it."

My mind is racing. Earl is here. I'm not sure why, but the whole idea of Earl Cochrane living and breathing in 1957 is filling me with dread. It just seems ... dangerous.

I push the thought away. Time is ticking, both here and in my own time, and I've got little of it left before the corporate client shows up. I need to know what Henry can tell me about closing. I need to get Henry away from the party.

"Did my ... cousin also tell you he's a car buff? He'd probably love a look at that Packard of yours."

Earl's smile dims a little. He's suspicious. But I can tell he's curious too.

Henry surveys the busy lot. "What the hell," he says. "Hard to turn down a request like that! I'm sure they can do without me for a few minutes."

He takes a swig from his beer, then turns and leads us around the corner of the building.

Earl and I trail behind. As Henry stops to shake a few hands, Earl tucks in close beside me.

"I know we've had some differences," he says in a low voice, "but this is bigger than all that. I've got plans. Do you realize what this means?"

"No, Earl. I don't."

"Do you know who won the 1957 World Series?"

"No, Earl."

"Do you know the stock price of Coca-Cola right now?"

"No."

"Me neither. But we can find out. We can make a fortune. Billions of dollars. More than any college degree can get you."

I think back to the gouged doorframe. The shave that ended in tragedy. The potential consequences of changing things in the past.

Earl Cochrane in 1957 is definitely a bad idea.

"I'm here to ask Henry a few questions, that's all," I hiss at him. "And then you and I are heading back to our time."

What I don't tell him is that we're also getting rid of the damn projector when we get there.

Before Earl can argue with me, Henry stops in

front of the gleaming Packard. "Here she is, boys. One of less than one hundred ever made."

Even Earl is taken aback by the car. He knows what I know—that this car might sell for a quarter of a million dollars in our time. I can see his wheels turning.

I need to take control of this conversation.

"Tell him about the deal you got on it," I say to Henry.

"I practically stole it," Henry says to Earl.

"I guess the guy wasn't much of a closer," I say.

Henry laughs. "Kid, there's no such thing."

I'm happy the conversation is shifting to where it needs to be, but Henry's caught me off guard. What does he mean there's no such thing as a closer? That's what I'm here for. I need to become one. Like . . . now.

"No such thing? Isn't that our job?" I ask.

My question sobers Henry instantly, and I see him reach for the whistle around his neck. "What did I tell you your job was, kid? The first shift? Move from selling to solving."

"Right. But . . ." I fumble to find a way to explain what I mean. "I still thought, you know, that you'd have to close the sale."

Henry shakes his head in mock frustration. "Are all your cousins this thick?" he asks Earl.

"No, sir," Earl says with a grin. "Just this one."

I roll my eyes at him.

"Look, kid. Everything I've been telling you is about creating trust," Henry says. "Building a relationship. If you want the sale to happen, then you need to go the extra mile. You need to take that relationship a step further."

"And what's that extra step?"

"Okay. First, let's review. Shift one—you've changed your approach to the job. From selling to solving."

"Right."

"Shift two is about changing your approach to the customer. From confrontation to collaboration."

"Roger."

"Shift three is using questions to uncover their problem. Changing from pitching to probing."

I can see Earl is really tuning in now. He's stopped pouring over every inch of the Packard and is leaning in, listening.

"And fourth gear is about adding value. Shifting from getting to giving."

I nod. "So that leaves us at fifth gear."

"Right. That's the final shift. From closing to coaching."

"Coaching?"

Why am I not surprised?

"Yep," Henry says, pointing his whistle at me. "You've built a relationship with the customer. You understand their problem. Now it's time to give them some advice. Help them make a great choice that they can feel confident in."

"But how will I know they'll take my advice?"

"If you've listened to them and understood their problem, and if you've done it in the spirit of giving, not getting, then they'll know you're not leading them on."

"And that will close them?"

Earl leans in another inch.

"No!" Henry throws his arms up in the air. "I told you there's no such thing as closing someone!"

I don't know if it's the beer or just his passion for the job, but he's on the verge of yelling.

"You can't close a sale. You can't close people." He stabs his whistle into my chest, punctuating each word. "You. Can't. Close. Anything."

I stand in quiet shock. Even Earl is wide-eyed.

Henry calms himself. "Look, kid. Just remember this, and you'll be fine. You can't close people. They close themselves."

It's like someone just opened a window. Suddenly it all makes sense.

"I get it," I blurt out. "It's like coming full circle. My job isn't to sell, so why would it be to close? People do that themselves. I just . . . I just . . ." I fumble for the right words. "I just coach them through the process."

A huge grin creeps onto Henry's face. He holds up the silver whistle and shakes it in triumph. Then, he does something I've never seen him do before.

He winks at me.

"That's all you need to know, kid."

I can tell Earl isn't buying Henry's approach in the same way I am. He's just opened his mouth, about to argue the point, when we're interrupted.

A young boy races around the corner of the building, a metal wagon in tow. It's Alan. He pulls up short when he sees Henry.

"Ah. Here's my boy." For the second time today, I notice Henry is in a remarkably cheerful mood. He downs the last of his beer and looks at his watch. "Which reminds me. I've gotta run home and pick up Mrs. Langford. She'll have my hide if she misses this party. I should probably take Alan here with me."

Alan beams. I suspect this is a rare moment for him to spend time alone with his father, and I'm briefly cheered by the thought.

Then I realize.

This is it. Henry's leaving. In the Packard. For the last time. This is the drive. The one that kills him.

And he wants to take Alan.

Is that supposed to happen? What if the only reason that Alan came around the corner to find his dad here is because we got Henry talking? Am I about to kill a young boy because I wanted to learn how to sell cars?

My heart begins to pound.

"You can't!" I blurt out.

Earl looks at me, bewildered.

"I mean . . . it's a beautiful day." I lean in toward Henry. "Maybe you want to have a nice romantic drive with Mrs. Langford? Alone? Alan can stay with me."

Henry ponders this for a moment, then shrugs. "Sure. I'll be back in twenty minutes anyway." He turns to Alan. "Going to get your mother, son. See you soon."

I can see the disappointment in Alan's eyes. He gives me a dark look, then turns and drags his wagon slowly around the corner. It's a painful thing to watch—but not as painful as what might have happened.

This time travel business is tricky indeed.

Henry gets in the car and starts the big engine.

"Kid," he calls out to me.

I step over to the driver's side door.

"Yeah?"

"You did good this week. Your paycheck's in the office."

He puts the car in gear, and Earl and I watch as Henry roars out of the parking lot.

I smile. I hadn't even thought about a paycheck.

Then my smile fades. I realize that Henry is driving for the last time. I never had a chance to say goodbye.

I watch the gleaming Packard as it disappears into the distance.

I turn to Earl. "Let's go home."

FIFTH GEAR

The Shift: From Closing to Coaching

Customers close themselves when they feel heard, understood, and guided.

CHAPTER 9

THE LAST UP

It's the first time I've time traveled with someone else, but it seems to work just the same. To my surprise, Earl offers no resistance to traveling back to our time. He's eager, in fact, and follows me without complaint.

We arrive in the cellar, and I check my watch. By the time I lift my head, Earl is already heading for the stairs.

"When does he get here?" I call after him.

He stops and turns around. "Who?"

"Who? The corporate guy. What time is his appointment?"

Earl laughs. "Who cares? Why would I give a rat's ass about selling a few cars today when I can make millions back then? I go back there and buy a few stocks, and I'm set for life." He shakes his head and chuckles. "I don't know what they taught you in college, boy, but it sure didn't take."

Then he turns and bounds up the cellar steps and vanishes into the bright sunshine.

Jennifer sees me as I walk through the front door of the dealership and immediately hangs up the phone. "Where the heck have you been?" she hisses. "And where's Earl? The guy is here—he's on the lot."

I take a deep breath. "Earl's gone. I'm taking the guy by myself."

She makes no effort to hide her skepticism. "Really? Okay . . ."

"Thanks for the vote of confidence. Really. That's a big help."

"Sorry. It's just, well . . . you're not exactly our leading closer right now."

I think back to Henry's near-tantrum about closing. Or not closing, as the case may be.

The Henry who's dying right now.

Only . . . that's not right. He died decades ago. I

know that. It just feels like now.

"Don't worry," I tell Jennifer. "Customers close themselves."

"Whatever you say, Mark," she says. "Just don't screw it up."

"Great."

"That wasn't from me. That was from Alan. He called and said, 'Tell him not to screw it up.'"

Fantastic.

The weather has finally broken. The lot is cooler than it's been in days. I could even be pretty comfortable in the gorilla suit right now, but I'm confident those days are behind me. In fact, this whole job could be behind me in just a few minutes if I mess this up.

Even from a distance, the guy looks serious. He's frowning at the sticker on a car near the front of the lot. And if I'm reading his body language right, it's telling me, "Get lost."

Don't panic. I tell myself. He's here because he already wants to buy.

He looks up as I approach. I stick out my hand. "Mark Dunham," I say. "Welcome to Langford."

"Carl Huxton," he says warily, returning my handshake. "You my new sales guy?"

I'm about to say yes, but I can tell he's squaring off

against me already. I just got here, but we're already on opposing teams, and he's calling me the sales guy. I've blown the first two shifts already, and all I've done is tell him my name.

Henry's voice rings in my ear. People don't want to be sold. A sale is what happens after you solve someone's problem.

"We save that title for the guys in the gorilla suits and cowboy boots," I blurt out.

His eyes widen, and then he almost smiles. "Well, I have seen a few of those types in my day."

"Think of me as . . . your coach," I say.

He looks at me quizzically, as if he's rolling the idea around. Trying it on for size. Then he turns his attention back to the car in front of us. "I guess you want to take me on a test drive," he says, and I swear he almost sighs.

A week ago, I would have shouted, "Yes!" and tried not to high-five Trevor as I sprinted for the keys. But something tells me to hold off. A voice in my head is starting to ask questions.

What's strange is that it's not Henry's voice I hear. I think it's mine.

What's the problem this guy is facing? How is a test drive going to solve it?

I take a deep breath.

"Mr. Huxton, are you ever going to drive this car?"

He looks up at me. "No. These will all be driven by sales reps and our follow-up service teams. I'm a purchaser."

"So your job is to buy the cars, not drive them."

He pauses. Just for a moment. "That's correct," he says slowly.

I turn and lean back against the car, lost in thought. *What's the problem?* the voice says again.

"Well. You must have gone through all this plenty of times before. How many places have you done this?" I ask.

"In almost every state."

"Even Hawaii?"

This time, he actually does smile. "No. But I've been pushing for a branch office there since the day I started," he jokes.

I grin. "I bet. So how does it work? You go wherever they open a new branch?"

"Once they get through the HR stage, they find an office location, and I get called in. There's a lot of purchasing in a new office. My job, among other things, is to show up at the new location and buy a fleet of cars."

"Why not arrange some sponsorship deal with a

manufacturer? You know, something nationwide?"

Carl relaxed his stance. I can tell he's getting into his comfort zone. "Head office says we have to buy local. To be honest—and no offense—it's a real pain in the ass."

You're close, says the voice. *Close.*

"How come? It seems to me that if you're buying two dozen vehicles at a time, you could pretty much pick a car, state your terms, and have them delivered wherever you like."

"That's true," he says. "I do have a lot of buying power." He pauses, as if considering something. "But that power comes with a lot of responsibility. If I buy two dozen lemons, that's a black mark on my name."

"That ever happen?"

He thinks for a moment. "Well ... no. They make cars pretty well in general. I can probably buy anything off this lot and it'll run great for a few years. Most things that might go wrong in that time period are covered."

My mental wheels are turning.

"So," I say after a pause, "you can pretty much name your price, and you can pretty much pick any model on the lot?"

He shrugs, but I can see I'm right.

"Then what holds you back? What stops you when the time comes to decide?"

He looks at me for a long moment.

"That," he finally says, "is a very good question. Most of the time, everything goes smoothly. Occasionally, a dealer will promise me cars, and then they don't show up. But the bigger problem has been that I can't get the service after the sale. I need these cars to stay on the road. Every day a car is down costs a few thousand dollars in this business. Three times now I've had dealerships go under or change hands, and I can't get the service."

Bingo.

I feel like I've just found a buried treasure. I take a moment. Collect my thoughts.

"So," I say, "is the pressure on you to find the right car or to find the right dealership?"

He looks at me, surprised again.

"The dealership. To be honest, the cars just don't matter that much."

I nod and look around the lot.

"Why don't we head inside?" I say. "There's no point in standing around looking at cars you're never going to drive."

I hold the front door open for Carl and follow him

through. Jennifer flashes him a welcoming smile, then raises her eyebrows at me. I ignore her.

"Cup of coffee?" I ask.

"Thank you."

I lead the way toward the tiny alcove that serves as a staff kitchen, but I take the long, slow route. There's something I need him to see.

Every wall in this place has photos of the dealership on it. Shots of Henry. Community events. Team pictures. You can't help but look at them.

And Carl doesn't disappoint.

"Who's this guy?" he asks, pointing at Henry poised above a dunk tank.

"Henry Langford. He founded this place after the Second World War."

Carl doesn't reply, but I know he's taking mental notes.

I point to another shot. "This is his son, Alan. He runs the place now."

"That's a lot of history," he says, absently.

We've made it to the coffee maker. From here, I can see him looking in Alan's office door at the photo above the desk.

"That's Henry with a 1950 Packard Custom Eight," I say. "Quite a character. He loved cars. Loved the business."

"He still alive? Sounds like you've met him."

"Uh . . . no." I feel a pang of sadness. "He died a long time ago. But . . . there are a lot of stories around here. A lot of history, as you say. Henry's still a big part of our culture."

"I can see that."

I hand Carl a cup of coffee and pour one for myself before we wander back to the showroom. He looks at the odd vehicle here and there and asks a few questions, but I can tell he's far more intrigued by the history of the dealership. The walls are covered with customer letters and testimonials, and I wait patiently as he reads one after another.

He meets all the staff, although Earl is still conspicuously absent, and we talk over a few details about delivery and his specific needs.

After almost an hour, I can tell the visit is winding down. I know I need to wrap things up somehow.

You can't close him, the voice says. He'll close himself if he feels he's been understood, and if you guide him to a good solution.

"Mr. Huxton," I begin, "we can easily supply your vehicles. You don't spend this long in the business without having good access to inventory. The real question is, are you comfortable we can meet your service needs after the fact?"

He takes a last sip of his coffee. "I think your little history tour has proven that, Mark. You've clearly got a stable business here."

"If you choose Langford, can you see us keeping your cars on the road?"

Even as I ask the question, I'm feeling pumped. I'm about to shift into fifth gear.

This is it!

Carl ponders the question, but only for a moment.

"I can't see why not," he replies.

I feel a surge of elation, and my stomach flip-flops with excitement. My mind begins to race forward as I envision telling the story to the rest of the team. My very own comeback tale of rising from the verge of joblessness to the biggest single sale in the history of Langford Auto. I look to Carl and smile, awaiting his confirmation.

And then . . . nothing happens.

I have this vague sense that Carl is waiting for something too, but I don't know what it is. I feel my stomach drop.

"Thanks for your time and your help, Mark," he finally says.

Then hands me his coffee cup and leaves.

CHAPTER 10
PAYDAY

I spend the afternoon in a funk. Either my gloom is contagious or the entire dealership is disappointed in me. I suspect it's a bit of both.

I don't understand what went wrong. I thought I'd nailed every step of the process: from finding the problem to offering a custom-fit solution. And yet he walked away.

It occurs to me to travel back to 1957 once more for help, but each time I think it, I remember that Henry Langford is dead. He's taught me everything he can.

For the rest of the day, whenever I'm not angry with myself for blowing the deal, I'm struggling with a huge sense of loss. Henry is gone.

My brain understands that he died long before I was born, but in my heart, it just happened. I feel like I should be attending a memorial service, but I'd be more than half a century late.

I'm so absorbed in my own pity party that I don't realize that there's someone standing at my desk. It's Trevor.

"Have you seen Earl?" he asks. "He's supposed to be on the lot right now, but I can't find him." Earl. I'd forgotten about him.

I have to believe he was serious about going back to 1957 to make money. How much preparation would he have needed? Could he already be back there?

"Um ... haven't seen him," I say. I look at my watch. "I have to go. I'll be back in a bit."

I try my best to walk casually out the front door of the dealership, and as soon as I'm outside, I hurry around the building, haul open the cellar doors, and rush down the stairs.

Everything looks the same. I feel another pang of sadness at the sight of Coach Henry standing on his wrinkled cardboard base near the box of films.

What to do? If Earl has already gone back, then what happens if I take the projector and the films?

Will he be trapped in 1957?

But, I reason, the projector should still be in 1957. Right? My brain is starting to hurt again from trying to process the whole crazy idea of time travel.

I decide I have no choice. I unplug the projector, take the reels off, and pack up the film. I fold down the projector's arms and stuff the whole thing back in its box.

"Sorry, Hank," I say to Cardboard Henry.

I'm about to load the whole works back into the large cardboard box it came in, when I notice an envelope in the box of remaining films.

It's an old Langford envelope, yellowed with age, but still sealed. Unstamped.

It's got a name scrawled on the front. My name. My heart is hammering in my chest. This is a letter to me written in 1957.

It's bulky. There's more than just paper inside.

I look at Cardboard Henry in disbelief, then sit down beside him on a crate and gently break the envelope's seal. It crackles opens easily. I pull out two thin sheets of paper.

The first is a check. It's for seventeen dollars for the pay period ending my last day at Langford in 1957. I laugh out loud. I have a funny feeling it's not cashable.

The second piece of paper is a note, written on Langford stationery.

Kid,

Good work this week. You're a quick study. Unless I've misjudged you, you've probably got a good handle on the five shifts.

Those shifts will take you a long way—in most cases, all the way to a sale. But there's one more thing you need to remember: sometimes you have to ask for the order.

A good coach would never let an up walk away without giving them a recommendation and suggesting they take it. If you've made it through the five shifts, not only have you earned the right to do it, but it's your obligation as a coach and a problem-solver. It's the right thing to do.

I've been through the five shifts with you, and I'm not about to let you walk away either. Consider this both a recommendation and an invitation: join us here at Langford. You won't regret it.

Welcome aboard, kid. Here's to many more paychecks—and much larger ones, at that.

Your coach and friend,

Henry Langford

P.S. See the reverse for a refresher.

On the back is a list of every shift, from first gear to fifth, handwritten by Henry. I skim through them, thinking back to how much has happened in so little time.

I reread the note. *Your coach and friend.* I wonder if he felt the same way about our short time together as I did. Or if he just wrote that to everyone.

I'll never know.

I turn my attention back to the envelope. There's something bulky inside. I turn it upside down.

A silver whistle falls into my hand.

The irony of Henry's note hangs over me as I finish packing the box. I've just received a job offer in the past that I can't accept, while being on the verge of losing mine in the present.

To make it worse, I think Henry was right: I would have been happy at Langford in 1957. But I'll never get to find out.

I hoist the box to my chest; then I take one more look around the cellar.

"Goodbye, Henry," I whisper. Then I balance the box against one hip, pull the light string, and the cellar falls into darkness.

Outside, the sun is starting to drop toward the

horizon as I load the box into the back of my car. I think briefly about Earl, but there's little more I can do for him.

My eye falls on the car that Carl was looking at when I first approached him earlier in the day. I can't help but feel like I did everything right.

I climb into the driver's seat and feel the silver whistle in my pocket. I wonder what Henry would have done in that situation. I'm guessing he wouldn't have let a twenty-seven car deal walk out the front door in the first place.

I reach for the key, but my hand falls away as my thoughts echo back at me.

I fumble in my pocket for Henry's note and scan the first page. It's right there staring me in the face:

A good coach would never let an up walk away without giving them a recommendation and suggesting they take it.

I step out of the car and head back toward the office. Five minutes later, I'm on the phone.

I'm too nervous to sit down, so I pace in front of my desk, tethered by the phone cord like a battered kite.

"Mr. Huxton. It's Mark Dunham from Lang-ford Auto."

"Hello, Mark." I can't tell from his voice if he's happy to hear from me or not. I decide it's neither. Yet.

"I wanted to thank you for your time today and ask you a few short follow-up questions," I say, then move quickly on. "Was there anything about the car we looked at today that didn't appeal to you?"

"No. It was fine, Mark."

"Were you comfortable with me and the other staff at the dealership?"

"Of course."

"Do you have concerns about whether we can keep your fleet of vehicles on the road reliably?"

"Not after what I saw today. The dealership clearly has a long history."

I take a breath.

"If you're happy with us, the vehicle, and our track record, then unless I'm mistaken, I truly believe we're the right fit for you. My recommendation to you is that you go with us. I believe it's the right choice."

I pause, and I can hear my heart pounding. I feel like I'm being very forward. But at the same time, I know I'm speaking the truth. We truly are the best fit for him.

"If we can meet your price requirements," I continue, "which I'm confident we can, would you be willing to take my recommendation?"

There's a long pause. I feel like I'm standing on the edge of a cliff.

"After all that, I can't imagine why I wouldn't," Carl says.

***

Twenty minutes later, Alan pages me to his office. He's swivelled around in his chair, his back turned to me.

My eyes trail over the gouge in the doorframe, then up to the picture of Henry on the wall. What a week.

I clear my throat, and Alan turns his chair around.

"Congratulations," he says. "Carl Huxton just called with a PO. It's done."

Alan stands up with a big grin and shakes my hand. "He just had to work out a few details before confirming the order, but he said you closed him in no time. He was quite impressed with how well you understood his dilemma."

It's what I expected, but I'm still speechless.

"Well done, Mark. I have to admit I was a little uncertain about you, but you've really turned a corner in the last few days. I don't know where you pulled all this sales stuff from, but it certainly seems to have worked."

I look up at the picture of Henry on the wall. I'm not quite sure what to say, but suddenly I know what to do. I reach into my pocket.

"I was in the cellar the other day, and I . . . I found this. I think your dad used to wear it around the lot."

I reach out and hand him the whistle.

"Huh," Alan says, then smiles. "I'd forgotten all about this." He chuckles and his eyes drift as he thinks back. "He always fancied himself a coach."

He tosses the whistle into the air and catches it.

"Thanks, Mark. That's a nice memory. Find anything else interesting? No one's been down there in years."

I pause. "Nah. Just some old junk. A lot of cardboard." Then I remember.

"And this," I say. I reach into my back pocket and hand him the list of shifts. "Is that your dad's handwriting?"

He looks at the paper, then nods. "Yep. That's his scrawl, all right. I still stumble across it from time to time. It's like his ghost is still here."

"A friendly ghost?"

"Yeah. He was a good man, Mark."

I feel my throat close a little.

"Yeah. I bet he was."

Alan turns back to the list, one hand holding the paper, the other grasping the whistle.

I turn and leave quietly, and head outside.

It's my turn on point.

And you never know where the next up will come from.

CHAPTER 11
THE CHOICE

It's funny how the mind works.

We have these moments we think we'll never forget—moments that are so poignant, or so new, or so emotionally charged that we feel we'll wake up thinking about them every day for the rest of our lives.

And then we don't.

We don't forget them—not the really important ones, anyway—but we don't re-live them every day, either.

Until we're reminded, of course.

On the northwest side of the city, there's a low hill

that juts out of the surrounding forest like a slowly balding head. You can see it clearly from the highway, and we pass it every time we visit Charlotte's parents—a trip that happens a lot more now than it used to.

For most of the year, that hill is a bare, mown strip of grass. Unremarkable but for the fact that it's something to look at on a long stretch of undeveloped highway. You can see it from a mile or two away.

Twice a year, though, on long weekends in the spring and fall, you can see the hill coming from twice that distance. In fact, on a nice day, you'll see the glints of reflected sunlight long before you see the hill itself.

On those days, I'm tempted to stop. We never have yet. Partly because classic cars aren't my thing, really. But mostly because the hill is at that sweet spot in the drive when Henny's just fallen asleep, and Charlotte and I are enjoying a rare moment of just being. In those moments, I'm reluctant to interrupt by dragging her to a car auction.

Today, I catch the first glitter of sunlight early, and I cast a sidelong glance at Charlotte. She's starting to nod off herself, her head dipping with the sway of the car. I'm tempted to stop, but that would wake up both of them. So I don't.

But I do slow down.

The hill is crowded with people—I can see hundreds of car junkies milling among dozens of sparkling classic cars, all crowding the brow of the hill like turtles emerging from the depths to warm in the sun.

Closest to the peak, I see the Packard.

It's almost in the direct center of the hill. The king of the turtles, surrounded by its loyal subjects.

And I am, of course, reminded.

This Packard isn't *the* Packard. It's not Henry's. That was destroyed the day Henry died. But it is a Custom Eight. The hood is open, hinged on the passenger side to lift up sideways. The top is down, the beautiful sloping trunk finishing the classic lines.

It's not Henry's Packard, no. But in that moment, I'm transported back in my mind. A lot has happened since the last time I saw him drive away in that car.

There's the baby. I watched in wonder as she lay sleeping on Charlotte's chest in the hospital.

"We don't have a name," she said.

"How about Henrietta?" I suggested.

She rolled it over in her mind. "She'd be Henny. For short." Then a pause. "I like that."

And so it was.

There's the job. I kept it. And, using Henry's help, I got pretty good at it. Really good, actually. Turns out the old man was on to something after all.

After the fleet sale, there were others. I think at first, Alan thought it was just luck or simply the law of averages, but I kept selling. Henry's shifts gave me confidence, which helped, but it was more than that. The shifts worked.

There was the man I called The Tirekicker. He'd been to the lot so many times that we almost hired the damn guy. We'd all taken our shot with him, and in the end, the consensus was that he was just what we called him: a tirekicker. He was never going to drive away in a car unless we gave him one. It got to the point that we'd draw straws just to see who had to put up with him.

I drew the short straw a few days after my last visit with Henry. Out of sheer desperation more than anything else, I went back to Henry's first shift—from selling to solving.

It turned out The Tirekicker had a credit problem—one that no one had bothered to take the time to find out about. We were so busy seeing the guy as our problem that we never discovered his.

That day The Tirekicker stopped kicking and started driving.

Even so, I still wasn't convinced that the shifts had made the difference. Anybody could get lucky, right? But the next day, more proof arrived in the petite form of Ms. April—and she was most definitely a "mizz" not a miss or a missus.

She stormed the lot like it was the beach at Normandy. I tried to shake her hand, and she actually swatted it away. I'm not kidding. She was the most defensive person I've ever met.

My gut response was to tell her to hit the road, but I remembered Henry's second shift—from confrontation to collaboration—and I caught myself.

"I know," I told her. "I hate buying cars too. It always

makes me feel like I'm outnumbered."

She just kind of . . . stared at me. And all of the bluster went right out of her. Suddenly, we were on the same team. After that, she was fine—and she bought a nice mid-size that day too.

Things slowed down for a few days after that, and I figured my lucky streak was over. But just as I was starting to beat myself up again, I noticed that the other guys were also experiencing success.

I caught Rusty, the guy who never shut up about specs and features, asking questions like he was Sherlock Holmes. When a young couple showed up on the lot, frazzled and on the verge of a marital collapse, it was Rusty, of all people, who figured out their true problem.

They thought they were disagreeing on how much they should spend. It was Rusty's smart questions— shifting from pitching to probing—that showed them they were really arguing about leasing versus owning. It was a cash-flow problem, not a price problem.

Once he found that out, the rest was easy—we had at least half a dozen vehicles on the lot that fit.

Trevor, too, started finding his way. He was still as shy as ever, but he started to find ways to make that work for him. Henry's fourth shift—from getting to giving—was a ray of hope for Trevor. Once he started to look at sales as a way to give, his whole outlook changed. He used to dread every interaction. Now each up is a way for him to do even more of what he loves.

I think Trevor is our King of Value. He's so focused on making sure that people see the value in what they're getting that his customers drive off the lot like they just won the lottery.

Every customer of Trevor's, no matter what price they pay, feels like they got the best deal in the country.

For my part, I think I fell in love with the fifth shift— from closing to coaching—more than any other.

I'd never felt like much of a closer to begin with, but I loved the idea of coaching. Not like Henry, mind you, with the outfits and the whistle, but in a subtler way. I loved being a trusted advisor. Someone people could be honest with and know they were getting honest, unbiased support in return.

One day, a savvy middle-aged woman named Barbara arrived on the lot. She was as sharp as they come. Trouble was that she knew it. Everything I said, she'd twist it into something I was trying to sneak past her.

"You're just saying that to make the other car look cheaper. That's basic psychology," she'd say. Or, "You're trying to close me by making me think this is a limited-time offer."

It was making me nuts. Finally I did something I never dreamed I'd do—I told her I couldn't sell her a car. She looked like I'd slapped her face.

"Why not?" she demanded, her hand on her hip.

"Because that's not what we do here. We don't close people. We coach them so they get what's right for them. I don't want you walking out of here feeling closed. I want you driving out of here feeling thrilled."

Forty minutes later, she bought a car. And you know what? She paid more than she would have across town—and did it happily. If I'd had Henry's whistle in my hand, I would have blown it 'til my face turned purple.

I don't have the whistle, of course. Alan does. He wears it around his neck every day now. But whistle or not, the sales rolled on through that long Indian summer, and then kept on rolling long into the fall.

We had to replace the missing Earl almost right away, but it wasn't long before we needed even more help, and then more still. The last two years have been nothing short of amazing.

And not just at work. The day I made my first sale, and handed Henry's whistle to Alan, I left the lot intending to head straight home and tell Charlotte the good news.

Instead, I found myself heading out of town in the opposite direction. I was, I realized, driving the same road Henry and I had in the Packard just days before.

For all the euphoria I felt after the fleet deal, I felt a deep loss. Henry was dead—decades ago, yes. But for me, that long afternoon? It was like it had just happened.

I found some comfort on the road that day—just as Henry did, I suspect. But I found something even more important: I realized Henry's shifts didn't just have the power to save my job. They could save my marriage, change my life and alter the way I interact with everyone I encounter. In fact, I realized the shifts could be useful for anyone.

It turned out to be surprisingly simple to use Henry's principles at home. In fact, I was able to turn my confrontation with Charlotte into collaboration. But first I had to stop trying to convince her that everything was going to be just fine. By asking a few questions, and really listening to the answers, I began to see how truly frightened she was at the idea of becoming a parent. She wasn't really angry at me. She hadn't lost faith in me. Her problem was that she was scared.

I knew right then my job wasn't to sell her on anything. Instead I just needed to work on solving the immediate problem—to help her feel safe.

Certainly, the fleet sale gave her some confidence. But the real turning point wasn't the sale or the money. It was my truly hearing her and understanding her fears that ultimately made her feel less afraid.

Once she felt safe, she started to open up to the idea that no matter what happened, we were going to face it together. Now we were on the same team. No matter what happened, she wouldn't be alone.

What also surprised me was how quickly I used the shifts to transform my relationship with my father-in-law, Gordon. For the entire time I had known him, I'd been pitching him something. I pitched him on letting me marry his daughter. I pitched him on investing in a hair-brained start-up idea I once had. I pitched him on getting me the job at Langford.

Once I shifted from pitching to probing, my stock started to rise in Gordon's eyes. I would ask him about what was happening at his dealership, about the challenges he faced growing and sustaining his business, about his strategies for being a great father, and about what makes him an effective leader. Let's just say he ate it all up, and I learned a lot in the process. He could tell that I was genuinely interested in what he had to say, and the result was that he started asking for my input.

This is a Gordon who only emerged after I started using the shifts. I'd risen from disappointing son-in-law to something different in his eyes. Part of that is Henny, certainly. But I suspect the shifts and my success at Langford have just as much to do with it, if not more.

Another part of it, I admit, is that I've come to appreciate him more too. Working in sales has given me a better understanding of what Gord has built.

Being in sales is difficult, and you don't get good at it without effort and help.

I've had both.

This awareness helped me shift right into fourth gear. I started giving input and ideas, and he started respecting me for the value I brought to the relationship. I never mentioned my secret source of wisdom because Gordon was never much of a sci-fi fan, but he didn't seem to care where my newfound curiosity or value came from; he was just happy to have me around.

Over time I even started to believe that Earl could have benefited from the shifts. He really wasn't all that bad of a person. He was just misguided. The guy was a closer. He had a closer's mindset and a closer's take-it-or-leave-it attitude. In turn, he was closed off to the world and all the joy life has to offer. If he could have made the fifth shift things may have turned out a lot different for him.

Had he been able to make the shift from closing to coaching he may have discovered the wonder, the excitement and the emotional rewards I've experienced from coaching others.

In order to make the shift, he would have had to

stop trying so hard to force his own agenda on others and instead start sharing his knowledge and experience. If he would have been more open and taught others the lessons he'd learned over the years, he would have found more fulfillment—not only at the dealership, but in his whole life.

Hank told me that once I got the shifts, everything else would be easy.

He was right, but—

—A horn blares behind me, and I realize I've slowed to a crawl, lost in my daydream.

I put my foot down on the gas, and in my mind, I briefly hear the roar of the Packard when Henry stepped on it. And then the hill is past, and the daydream is over.

Charlotte and Henny both sleep for the rest of the drive, and I savor the time, enjoying both the solitude, and a moment of gratitude for how truly well things turned out.

***

Charlotte stirs beside me as we pull into the long

driveway. "Already?" she mumbles, as she undoes her seatbelt.

We collect Henny—along with the multitude of things that need to travel with her everywhere—and head for the house. The door opens before we're even partway up the walk, and Charlotte's mother appears, cooing over Henrietta and ushering Charlotte into their huge home.

"Gordon's out back," she calls to me. "He's waiting for you."

I head through the house and out onto the back patio, where I find Gord, holding court with a group of men I've never seen before.

"Mark," he booms. "Great to see you. Great." He clamps firmly onto my hand and looks me square in the eye. It's now his new normal—he is actually glad to see me.

I look around the circle of faces.

"Mark, these are my regional managers," Gord tells me. "We had a meeting this morning, and they're on their way back home soon."

They all stand up, I shake everyone's hands, and we introduce ourselves.

Then they all sit back down. It doesn't seem like

they're on their way home any time soon. In fact, if I'm reading this right, they seem like they're waiting for something.

It turns out I am reading it right.

"I was just telling these guys how you've transformed your dealership," Gord says. "I'm really impressed with the work you've done. Alan tells me you've got some secret formula for your guys—some five-step plan. Whatever it is," he gives me a knowing smile, "I know you're one hell of closer. And," he adds, "you've worked damn hard from what I hear."

This is high praise coming from Gord.

"Thanks," I say. "But, I really can't take all the credit."

If he only knew how true that was.

Gord laughs and turns to his team. "Didn't I tell you he'd say that? Didn't I tell you?" He claps me on the shoulder again. "You never let me down, Mark."

I'm certain this is not true. But I'm also certain that, in this moment, Gord believes what he's saying. And that's enough for me.

Gord hands me a beer. It's 11:00 in the morning, and I raise an eyebrow, but accept. There's clearly something going on here.

"Mark," Gord begins, addressing the entire group

as much as me, "I'd like to make you an offer."

***

My mind is swirling on the way home.

Gord has just offered me an incredible opportunity. Sales manager for his flagship dealership is a big deal. It's good money at a high volume dealership. I'd be set.

And I'm no dummy. I know what this job really is.

Gord's not getting any younger. Charlotte is his only child. But she's seen enough of the car business to last a lifetime.

Nope. This isn't just about a sales manager job.

Gordon is grooming me to take over the whole thing.

It's a golden opportunity. I'd be set for life. Charlotte would be thrilled.

There's just one problem.

Alan's offered me the same thing.

***

I'm so preoccupied on the trip home that I'm almost right on top of the cop car before I see it. Charlotte grabs my arm, and I slam on the brakes.

There's a cop standing on the highway beside his cruiser. He's hot. Sweaty. Grumpy. The cruiser lights are flashing, and he's waving an orange baton to direct traffic off the highway. We're being rerouted.

We're almost at the site of the car auction, and for a moment, I'm convinced I'll see the Packard from this morning, twisted in a heap in the ditch, surrounded by flashing lights. Like some weird Karmic dent in the universe that I've created by messing around in 1957.

But it's just construction.

The detour takes us east, then south, and we're driving through an older part of the city that I haven't been to in years. That's not surprising—this neighborhood doesn't have much to offer.

We slowly crawl along the bumpy streets, past industrial supply houses, small manufacturing buildings, and the odd bar or restaurant. More than anything, though, we're passing vacant buildings. The whole area feels steeped in desperation.

There's movement ahead, and I refocus on the road. Someone is standing on the sidewalk waving their arms.

Only it's not a someone.

It's a something.

For a moment, I can't believe what I'm seeing. I refuse to accept it.

I'm vaguely aware that the car has stopped moving. I haven't used the brakes. I've just . . . stopped driving and we've rolled to a halt.

The thing stops waving its arms. When I don't do anything but stare, the thing turns its attention back to the traffic and begins waving again.

The thing is a gorilla. Or, more accurately, it's someone in a gorilla suit. And the gorilla is wearing—I kid you not—a plaid sports coat.

I look to my right, and at that moment, I feel my vision darken around the edges.

"Mark?" Charlotte rests her hand on my arm, concerned.

I don't answer. I can't answer.

I've stopped the car in front of a used car lot. One that may have seen better days, but almost certainly hasn't seen many worse. The cars are cheap, older models. Driven hard. The office is a run-down building that someone has recently tried to paint, but it's still a pig in lipstick no matter how much you squint.

None of that, of course, really matters. It's a barely-getting-by car lot. They have them in every city, every town.

What matters is the sign.

It sits precariously on the roof of the office, leering down at the lot like a dark, skeptical brow.

It says, "Cochrane Auto."

Cochrane as in Earl.

I look back at the gorilla. The gorilla in the plaid jacket.

It can't be. Earl would be ... well, he'd be dead. If he stayed in the 1950s to try his luck, the sheer passage of time would have gotten him by now.

Wouldn't it?

I shift the car into park and step out onto the sidewalk.

***

It's not Earl in the suit, of course. It's a young guy who's bought the business—what was left of it anyway—and is trying to make a go of it.

"The monkey costume came with the place," he says. "The coat too."

And the guy he bought it from?

"Never met him," he says. "He died. I bought it

from the bank. Manager told me he was a real S-O-B though. Miserable right to the end."

***

Funny thing about endings. When you reach them, you realize that you owe thanks to unexpected places and people.

After everything that's happened, it turns out that it's Earl, of all people, who helps me make the biggest decision of my career.

By the time we get home, I've already made up my mind. I won't be joining Gord's team. He'll be disappointed, but I think in the end, he'll respect me for it. It's better this way.

Why?

In the end, I've come full circle. From one gorilla suit to the next. Neither one of them worked. Neither of them sold cars. But they both served to show me that there's a way to sell that works, and that fits.

Learning what became of Earl. And seeing that kid in the suit—it's shown me that I can't take Gord's job because I don't want to wear the gorilla suit. Not even figuratively. My gorilla days are over.

I want to be part of a coaching culture. Not a selling one. A coaching culture is what Langford has. It's what Henry started, and I rediscovered, and what Alan and I are building now together.

Henry's shifts—the handwritten scrawl that now hangs in Alan's office—are more than just a way to sell. They're a way to be happy doing it. To be proud. And that's what I need more than anything else.

Henry taught me this: we're all ups at one time or another. And we all need a coach from time to time.

And when the two meet? It's just like magic.

THE END

FROM FIRST TO FIFTH:

FIRST GEAR
The Shift: From Selling to Solving

*Between every customer and every sale is a problem.
Your job is to identify the problem and solve it.*

SECOND GEAR
The Shift: From Confrontation to Collaboration

To discover your customer's problem, join their team.

THIRD GEAR
The Shift: From Pitching to Probing

*Asking questions shows genuine interest
and helps reveal the customer's true problem.*

FOURTH GEAR
The Shift: From Getting to Giving

*Giving real value allows you to
earn respect and sales.*

FIFTH GEAR
The Shift: From Closing to Coaching

*Customers close themselves when they
feel heard, understood, and guided.*

EPILOGUE

HOW TO MAKE A SHIFT IN ANY AREA OF YOUR LIFE

When we first imagined the world of Mark Dunham, Henry and Alan Langford, and Earl Cochrane, our goal was to help sales people. But as the story and the characters came to life—as we got to know their very real personalities and challenges—we realized that the five shifts are powerful tools for anyone, at work or at home.

Throughout our lives we're frequently asked

to "sell" ourselves or our ideas. We're expected to convince or persuade others. We're called on to effect change.

Every day, for example:

Parents want their children to use manners and show kindness and respect.

Job seekers want to score an interview and land the job.

Managers ask their team members to believe in them and to follow their directions.

Employees desire to be noticed, stand out and move up in the organization.

Teachers aim to sculpt the thinking of their students.

Students wish to be selected for a scholarship.

Social workers attempt to alter the course of people's lives by causing them to change their actions.

Leaders must cause others to believe in their vision and join them on their mission.

It turns out we're all selling in some way. But most of us were never taught to sell effectively and with dignity. The "shifts" of *The Last Up* are a tool for doing just that. By shifting from selling to solving, from confrontation to collaboration, from pitching to probing, from getting to giving, and from closing to coaching,